English Grammar Practice

Contents

1 The Alphabet 3
2 A – An 9
  Progress Check 1 (Units 1–2) 13

3 Numbers 15
4 Plurals 17
  Progress Check 2 (Units 3–4) 20

5 Personal Pronouns 22
6 The verb 'to be' 26
  Progress Check 3 (Units 5–6) 31

7 This / These – That / Those 33
8 'Have / Have got' 37
  Progress Check 4 (Units 7–8) 42

9 There is / There are 44
10 'Can' 48
   Progress Check 5 (Units 9–10) 53

11 Possessives 55
12 The Imperative 60
   Progress Check 6 (Units 11–12) 63

13 Present Continuous 65
14 Present Simple 70
   Progress Check 7 (Units 13–14) 79

15 Prepositions of Place 81
16 Prepositions of Time 85
17 Who – What 90
   Progress Check 8 (Units 15–17) 93

Revision

Revision 1 Units 1–2) 95
Revision 2 (Units 1–4) 97
Revision 3 (Units 1–6) 99
Revision 4 (Units 1–8) 101
Revision 5 (Units 1–10) 103
Revision 6 (Units 1–12) 105
Revision 7 (Units 1–14) 107
Revision 8 (Units 1–17) 109

Word List 111

Introduction

New Round-Up Starter English Grammar Practice combines games and fun with serious, systematic grammar practice. It is ideal for young learners in the preliminary stages of English language learning.

Students see grammar points clearly presented in colourful boxes and tables. They practise grammar through lively, highly illustrated games and oral and writing activities.

New Round-Up is especially designed for different students studying English in different ways.

It can be used:
- in class with a coursebook. Students do both oral work – in pairs and in groups – and written work in New Round-Up.
- after class. The 'write-in' activities are ideal for homework. Students can practise what they have learned in the classroom.
- on holidays for revision. New Round-Up has clear instructions and simple grammar boxes, so students can study at home without a teacher.

The New Round-Up Teacher's Book includes a full answer key, quizzes, tests plus answer keys, and audio scripts of progress check listening tasks.

The Alphabet

🎧 2 **Listen and repeat.**

A *A*

a *a*

apple

B *B*

b *b*

ball

C *C*

c *c*

cat

D *D*

d *d*

doll

E *E*

e *e*

egg

F *F*

f *f*

frog

🎧 3 **Sing along!**

A for apple   C for cat   E for egg
B for ball   D for doll F for frog

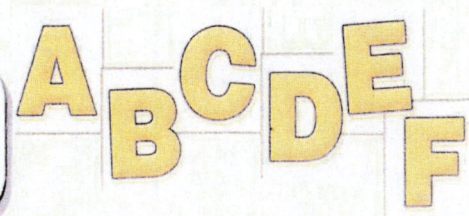

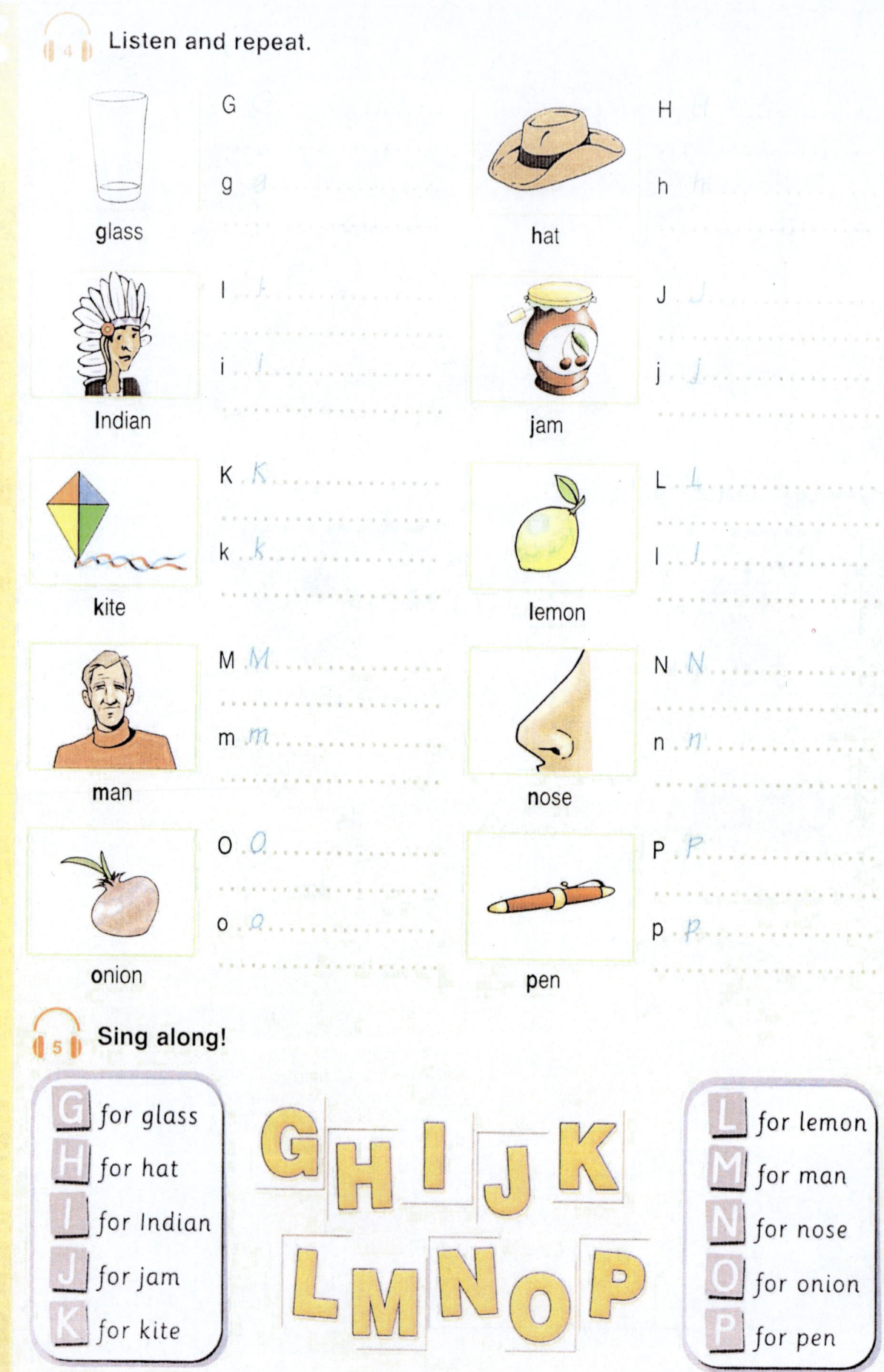

The Alphabet

6 Listen and repeat.

- queen — Q q
- star — S s
- umbrella — U u
- watch — W w
- yo-yo — Y y
- rain — R r
- train — T t
- van — V v
- box — X x
- zoo — Z z

7 Sing along!

Q for queen
R for rain
S for star
T for train
U for umbrella
V for van

Q R S T U
V W X Y Z

W for watch
X for box
Y for yo-yo
Z for zoo

I can learn it! You can too!

The Alphabet

1 Fill in the missing letters.

2 Look at the pictures. Look at the letters. Write the words.

1 ....doll....   2 ....   3 ....

4 ....   5 ....   6 ....

7 ....   8 ....   9 ....

The Alphabet

3 Fill in the missing small letters.

a b   d   f   h   j   l   n
p   r   t   v   x   z

4 Fill in the missing capital letters.

A B C   E   G   I   K   M   O
      Q   S   U   W   Y

5 Fill in the missing letters.

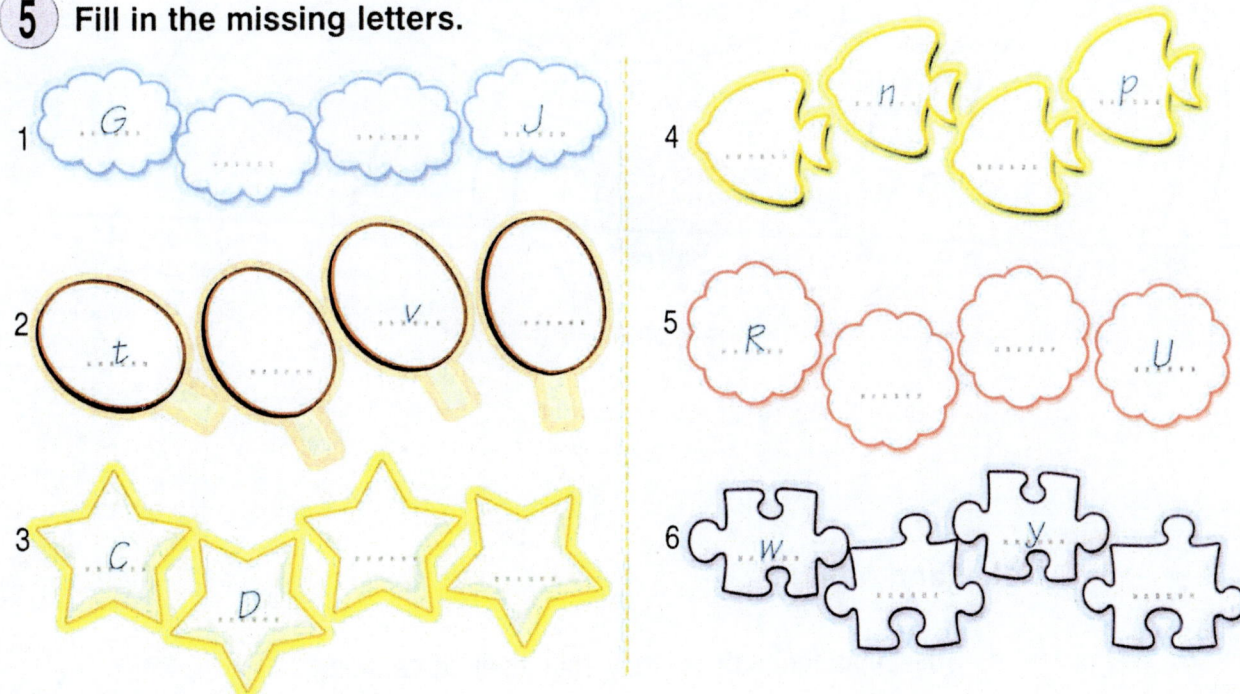

6 Write in capital letters.

1 dog	DOG	5 queen		9 cat	
2 apple		6 watch		10 glass	
3 umbrella		7 lemon			
4 jam		8 train			

7 Write in small letters.

1 CAT	cat	5 KITE		9 TRAIN	
2 EGG		6 ONION		10 FROG	
3 NOSE		7 ZOO			
4 YO-YO		8 PEN			

7

The Alphabet

8 Match the first letter of a word to the end of the word and its picture.

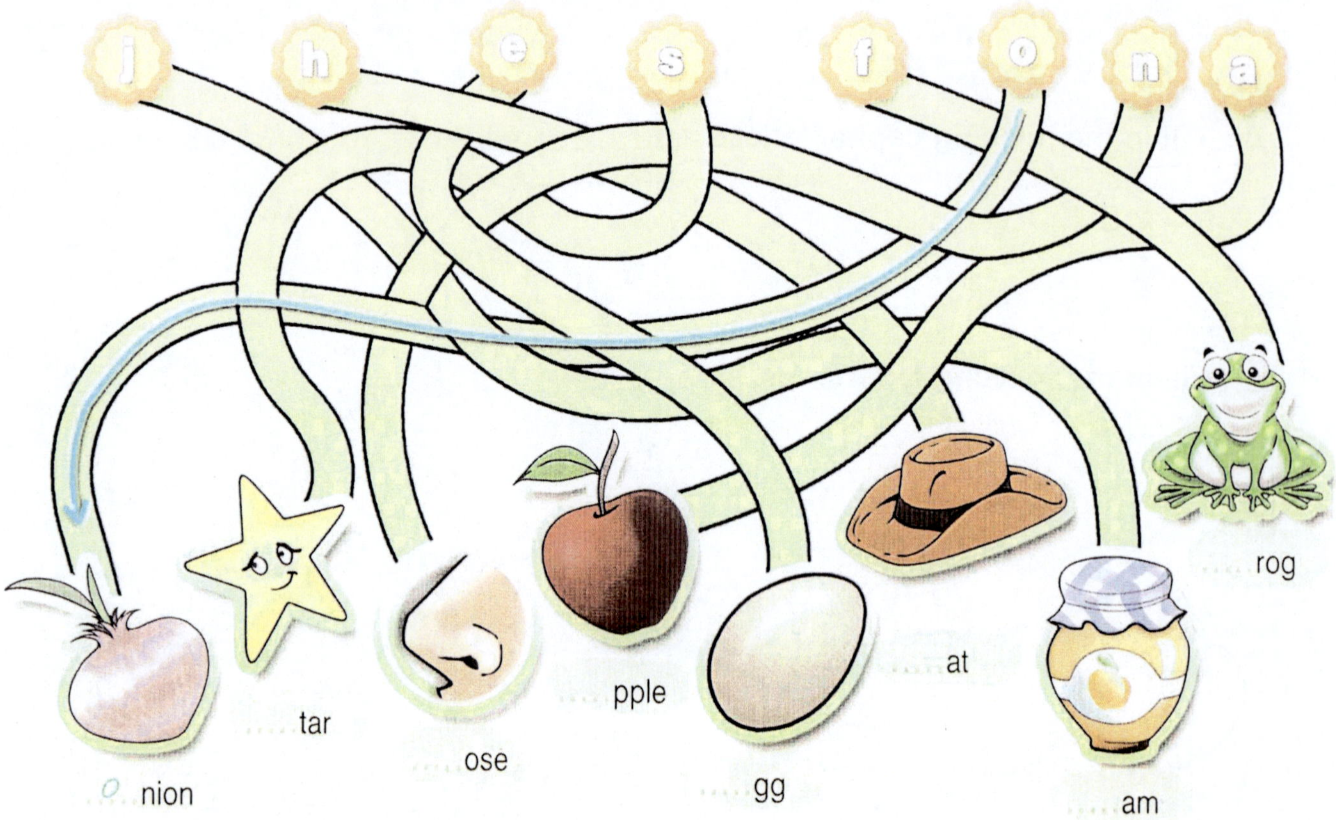

j   h   e   s   f   o   n   a

....rog
....tar
....pple
....ose
....gg
....at
....am
o. nion

9 🎧 Listen and repeat.

th /ð/ or /θ/	this, that, them, there, they, thin, thief, three, thing
ch /tʃ/	chart, cherry, chess, child, church, chin, chair
ph /f/	phone, photo, Philip
sh /ʃ/	ship, shop, shell, shut, shoe, shot

Alphabet Game

Student A: Say a letter.
Student B: Write the letter on the board.

B

8

A – An

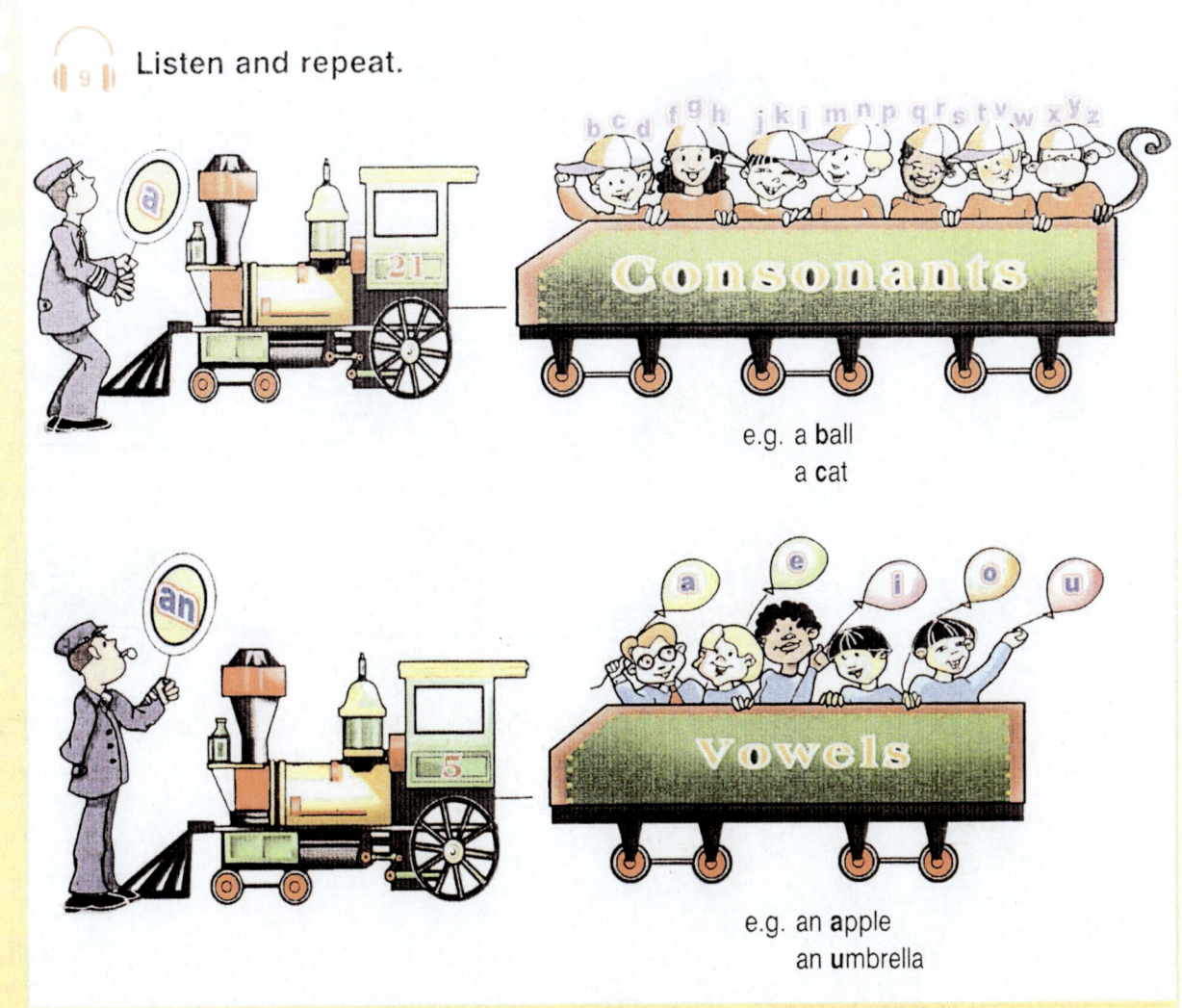

🎧 9 Listen and repeat.

e.g. a ball
     a cat

e.g. an apple
     an umbrella

1 Circle the vowels.

c d ⓐ g k i l m o
p q w e x s z u f

2 🎧 10 Listen and repeat.

a + ll /ɔː/	ball, call, small, all, tall, fall
e is silent at the end	make, bake, snake, cake, apple, kite
ee /iː/	bee, sheep, see, feet, seed, meet
oo /ʊ/ or /ɔː/	book, cook, good, pool, moon BUT: door, floor

A – An

3 Fill in: *a* or *an*.

1 *a* dog
2 .... elephant
3 .... zebra
4 .... ant
5 .... snake
6 .... frog
7 .... octopus
8 .... cow
9 .... insect
10 .... bird
11 .... lion
12 .... alligator
13 .... donkey
14 .... owl
15 .... mouse
16 .... sheep
17 .... fish
18 .... horse
19 .... ostrich
20 .... bee

4 🎧 **Listen and repeat.**

c + a, o, u /k/	**c**at, **c**ost, **c**up, **c**offee, **c**oat, **c**an
c + e, i, y /s/	**c**ell, **c**inema, **c**ycle, **c**ity, **c**ertain
k is not pronounced before n	**kn**it, **kn**ife, **kn**ow, **kn**ee
q + u /kw/	**qu**een, **qu**it, **qu**estion
y /j/ at the beginning	**y**es, **y**ellow, **y**acht
y /ɪ/ at the end /aɪ/ in one syllable words	Mar**y**, tid**y**, Sall**y**, cherr**y**, sk**y**, fl**y**, dr**y**, sp**y**, cr**y**
s /z/ between vowels	ro**s**e, clo**s**e, ri**s**e

5 🎧12 Write the words in the correct column. Listen and check. Listen and repeat.

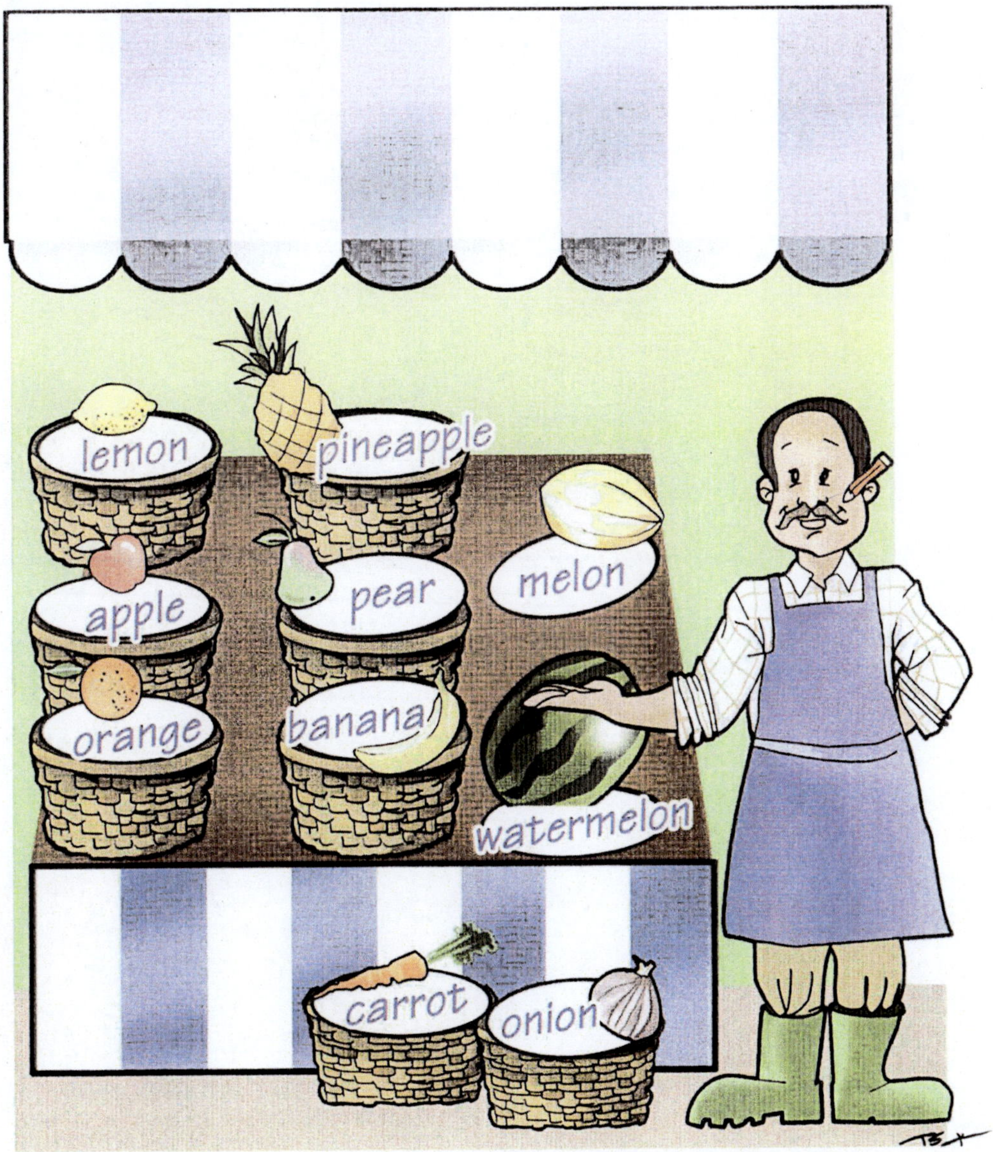

6 Circle the odd word out.

1 a mouse / cat / (owl)
2 an ant / donkey / elephant
3 an orange / lemon / apple
4 a umbrella / hat / girl
5 a pineapple / cake / ice cream
6 an horse / ostrich / ant

7 Fill in: *ball, apple, cat, egg, dog, frog, umbrella, box, yo-yo, queen, onion, glass, Indian, man, kite, pen.*

A – An

8 Fill in *a* or *an*.

1 ___ computer
2 ___ desk
3 ___ chair
4 ___ football
5 ___ bed
6 ___ umbrella
7 ___ robot
8 ___ cushion
9 ___ armchair
10 ___ envelope

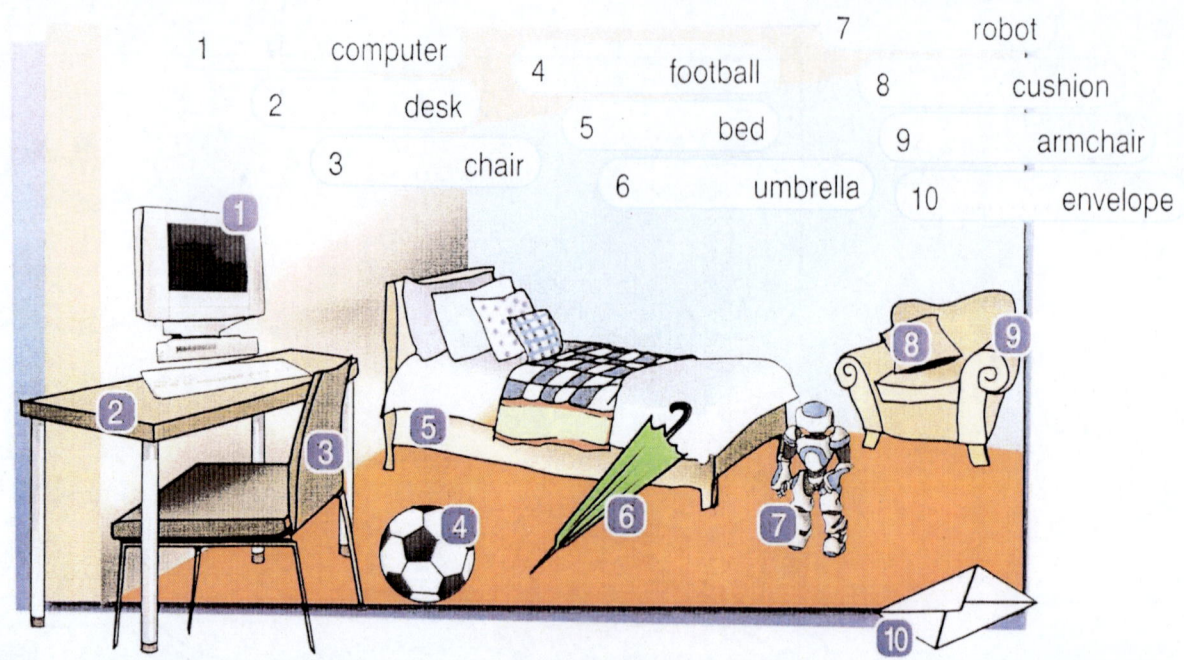

Speaking Activity

Student A: Say an animal from Ex. 3. Student B: Repeat adding *a* or *an*.

A or An?

 dog

 a dog

Writing Activity

Write a list of 6 animals we see in a zoo.

an owl ....
....

Remember?

Look at the picture in Ex. 8 for 2 minutes. Close your books. Can you remember all the things in the room?

1 Fill in the missing small letters.

2 Write the words in capitals.

cat   apple   ball   train

3 Look and write as in the example.

1 a star   2 ....   3 ....

4 ....   5 ....   6 ....

4 Read and circle.

1 a / an bird
2 a / an ant
3 a / an cow
4 a / an owl
5 a / an mouse
6 a / an horse
7 a / an alligator
8 a / an lion

5 Listen and draw lines. There is one example.

Pat   Ann   Kim   Tom   Ben   Sam

6 Song

Here's a doll
Here's a star
Here's an onion
Here's a car
Here's an egg
Here's a pen
Here's an apple
Sing again!

Here's a watch
Here's a hat
Here's an ostrich
Here's a cat
Here's an ant
Here's a bee
Here's a yo-yo
Sing with me!

Numbers

🎧 15 Listen and repeat.

| 1 one | 3 three | 5 five | 7 seven | 9 nine |
| 2 two | 4 four | 6 six | 8 eight | 10 ten |

1 Write the numbers.

🎧 16 Listen and repeat.

Numbers

Listen and repeat.

2. Help the bee go home. Write the missing numbers.

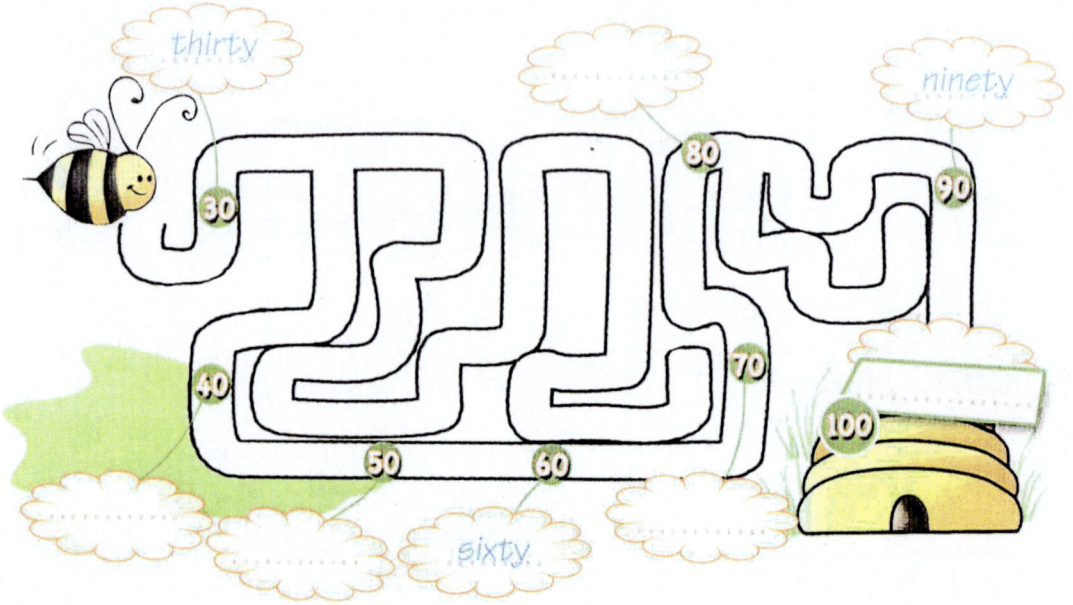

3. Write out the numbers.

1. 63 : sixty-three
2. 47 : ....
3. 55 : ....
4. 82 : ....
5. 91 : ....
6. 76 : ....

Find the numbers

Student A: Say a number. Student B: Say the number after it.

eleven

twelve

Plurals

🎧 18 **Listen and repeat.**

Singular — one flower
Plural — three flowers

Most nouns add -s.

1 Look and write.

1 .... two zebras ....
2 ....
3 ....
4 ....
5 ....

🎧 19 **Listen and repeat.**

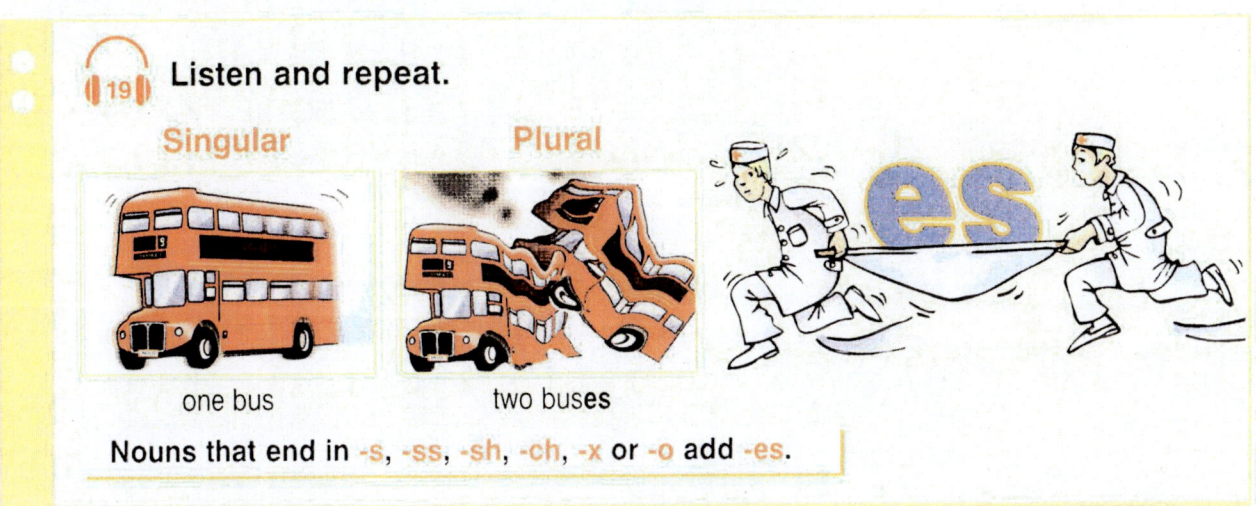

Singular — one bus
Plural — two buses

Nouns that end in -s, -ss, -sh, -ch, -x or -o add -es.

2 Write the plurals.

1 watch — watches
2 glass —
3 tomato —
4 brush —
5 box —
6 dish —

Plurals

🎧 20 Listen and repeat.

Singular — one baby
Plural — two babies
BUT
Singular — one toy
Plural — two toys

Nouns that end in consonant + **y** drop **y** and add **-ies**.

Nouns that end in a vowel (a, e, o, u) + **y** add **-s**.

3 Find the plurals of the words below in the puzzle.

baby, strawberry, boy, monkey, day, story, lady

A	E	S	L	M	O	L	A	D	I	E	S
L	M	T	O	E	A	S	I	L	M	Z	V
Y	M	O	N	K	E	Y	S	D	A	I	E
G	E	R	B	Y	S	T	O	E	K	B	O
J	Q	I	E	N	B	O	Y	S	T	A	F
S	G	E	O	D	A	Y	S	F	M	B	J
T	R	S	D	E	N	N	O	E	L	I	C
S	T	R	A	W	B	E	R	R	I	E	S
O	L	G	D	E	O	S	T	P	K	S	E

Pronunciation

We pronounce the ending of the plural form:

- /s/ when the noun ends in a(n) /f/, /k/, /p/, /t/ or /θ/ sound. chefs, parks, shops, bats, baths
- /ɪz/ when the noun ends in a(n) /s/, /ks/, /ʃ/, /tʃ/, /dʒ/ or /z/ sound. buses, foxes, dishes, witches, bridges, roses
- /z/ when the noun ends in all other sounds. toys, lemons, flowers, bags

4 🎧 21 Listen and tick (✓). Listen again and repeat.

	/s/	/z/	/ɪz/		/s/	/z/	/ɪz/		/s/	/z/	/ɪz/
rabbits				lorries				brushes			
boxes				oranges				hats			
planes				glasses				cars			

🎧 22 Listen and repeat.
Irregular Plurals

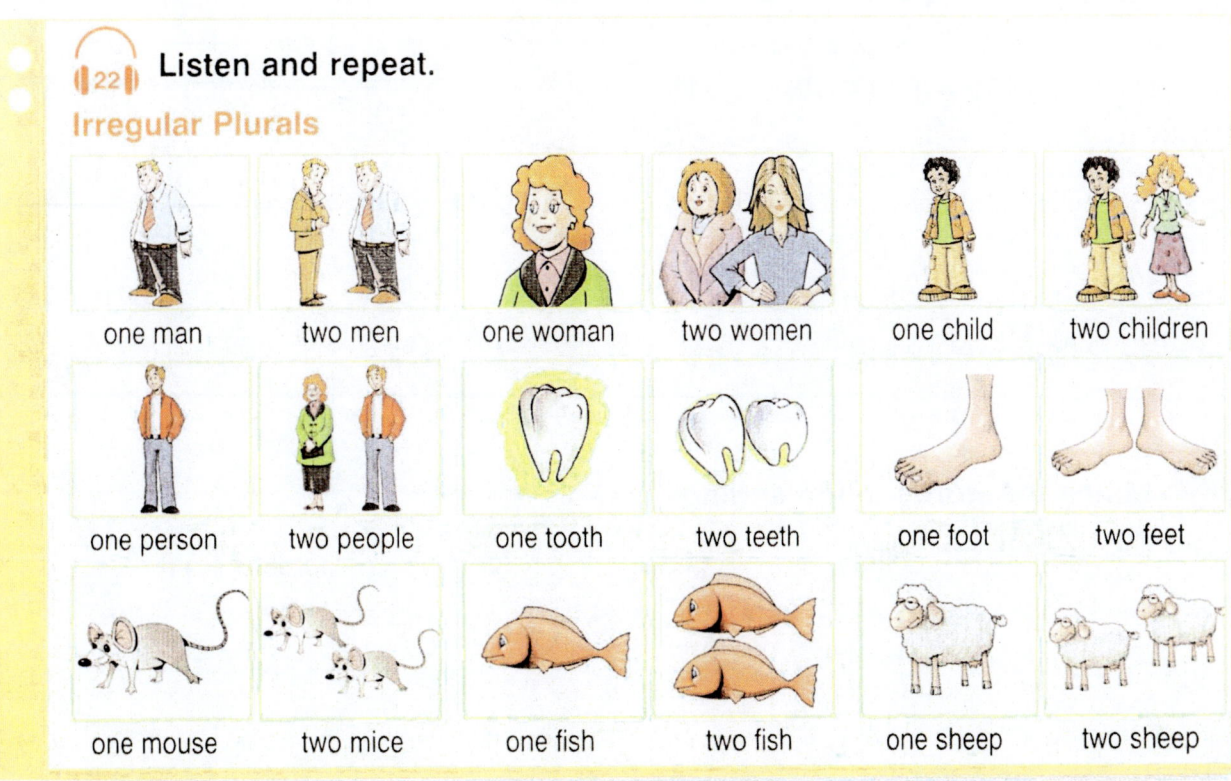

5 Count and write.

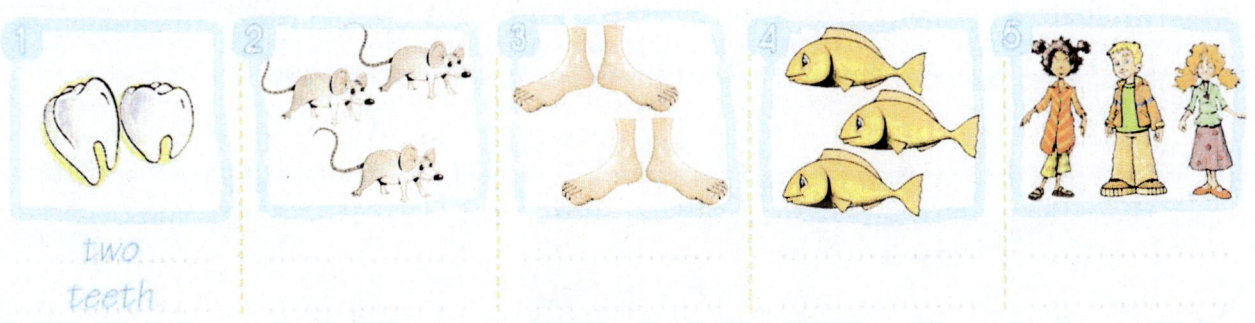

1. two teeth

Write the plurals

Student A: Say a word. Student B: Write the plural form on the board.
A: man   B: (writes) men

Progress Check 2 (Units 3-4)

1 Match the numbers to the words.

6   11   12   10   2   9   20   16

ten   six   eleven   nine   two   twelve   sixteen   twenty

2 Choose and circle.

1 30   thirteen   three   (thirty)   4 19   nine   ninety   nineteen
2 40   four   fourteen forty   5 7   seventeen   seven   seventy
3 15   fifty   fifteen five   6 80   eight   eighty   eighteen

3 Match the words to the endings.

lion   story   glass   lorry   tomato
zebra   lady   bus   boat

-s	-es	-ies
lions		

4 Look at the pictures. Look at the letters. Write the words.

1 ..... planes .....   2 ....   3 ....

                         5 ....   6 ....

5 Write the plurals.

1 child –
2 mouse –
3 man –
4 tooth –
5 sheep –
6 person –
7 foot –
8 woman –
9 fish –

Listening

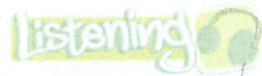

6 23 **Listen and write a name or a number. There are two examples.**

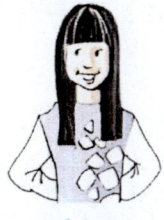

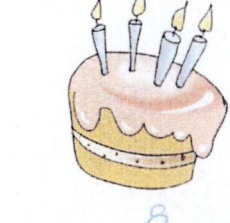

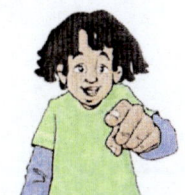

Lisa

8

1 ....

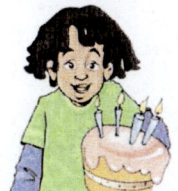

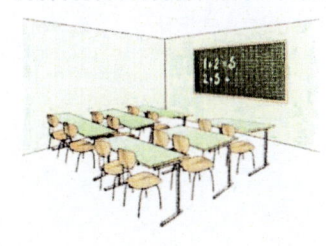

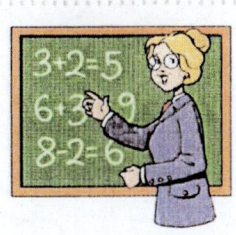

2 ....

3 ....

4 ....

7 24 Song

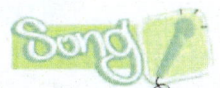

Two white sheep and three brown dogs
Four grey mice and five green frogs
Two red apples, three pink cakes
Four blue birds and five brown snakes
Lots of pictures in my book
Lots of pictures, come and look.

Two blue flowers, three green trees
Four black ants, five yellow bees
Two green vans and three white planes
Four red buses, five blue trains
Lots of pictures in my book
Lots of pictures, come and look.

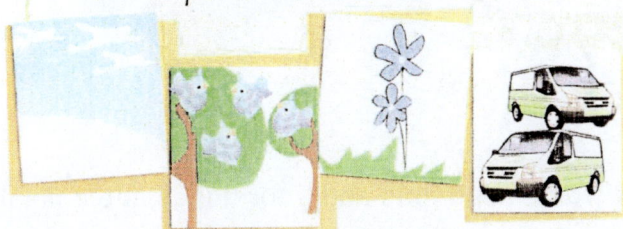

Personal Pronouns

🎧 25 Listen and repeat.

Singular	Plural
I	we
you	you
he, she, it	they

We say **he** for men and boys, **she** for women and girls and **it** for things and animals.

Personal Pronouns

1 Fill in: *I*, *he*, *she*, *it*, *we* or *they*.

2 Fill in: *he*, *she*, *it*, *we* or *they*.

1 Maria ..... *she* .....
2 hat ....
3 buses ....
4 you and I ....
5 boy ....
6 Carmen and Pedro .....
7 woman ....
8 Tom and I ....
9 frog ....

3 Match the correct pronouns to the pictures.

23

4 Read and circle.

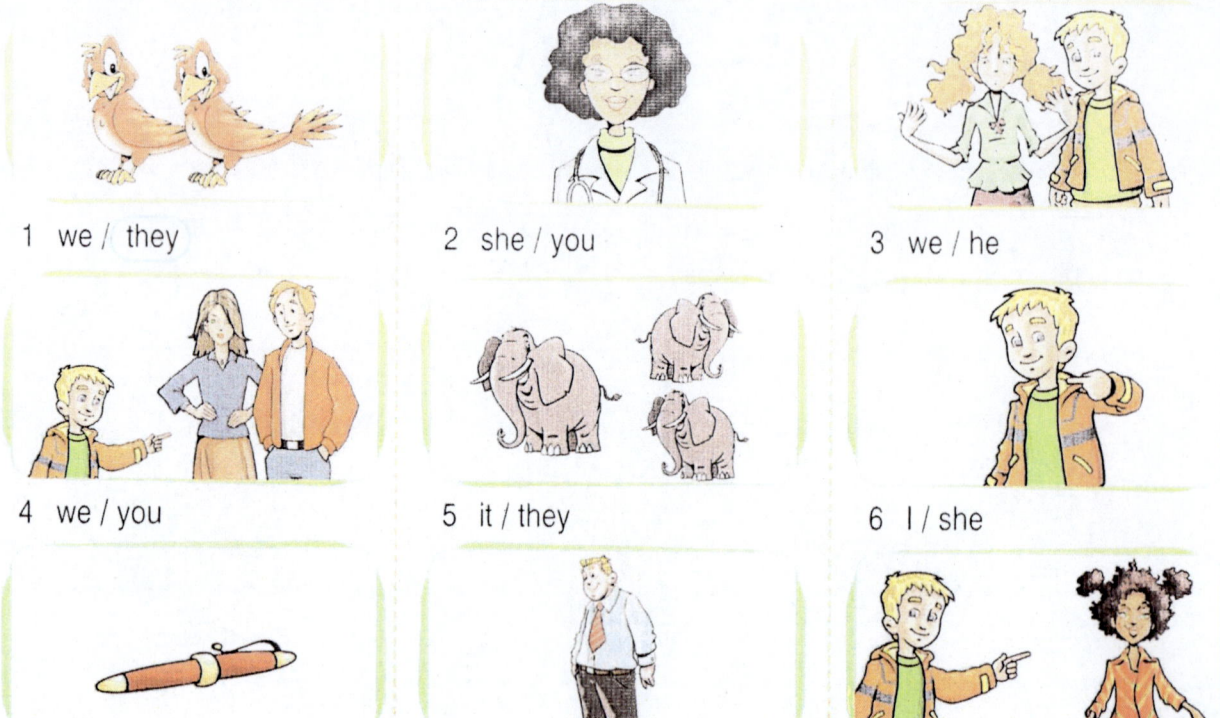

1 we / they

2 she / you

3 we / he

4 we / you

5 it / they

6 I / she

7 it / he

8 we / he

9 she / it

5 26 Write *I*, *you*, *he*, *she*, *it*, *we* or *they*. Listen and check.

1 ....

2 ....

3 ....

4 ....

5 ....

6 ....

7

8

9

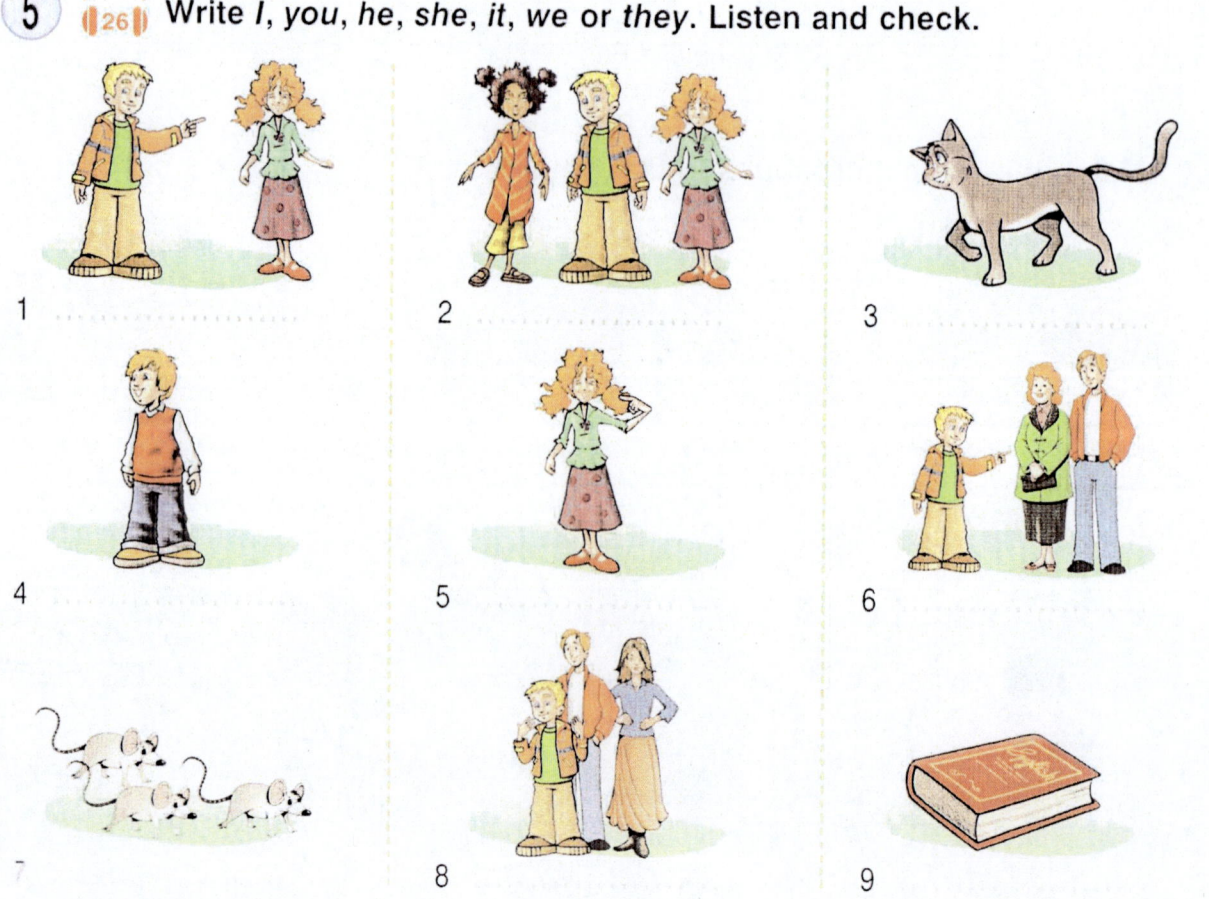

6 Write *he*, *she*, *it*, or *they*.

7 Match.

1 Jenny
2 a dog
3 Mum and Dad
4 Lucy and I
5 Ben
6 three monkeys
7 a boy
8 a yo-yo

a we
b it
c he
d she
e they
f it
g they
h he

Say the pronoun!

Work in pairs. Find a picture in the unit. Point to the picture. Your partner says the correct pronoun. Now, your partner finds a picture.

It

The verb 'to be'

  Listen and repeat.

Affirmative		Negative		Interrogative
Long form	Short Form	Long	Short Form	
I am	I'm	I am not	I'm not	Am I?
You are	You're	You are not	You aren't	Are you?
He is	He's	He is not	He isn't	Is he?
She is	She's	She is not	She isn't	Is she?
It is	It's	It is not	It isn't	Is it?
We are	We're	We are not	We aren't	Are we?
You are	You're	You are not	You aren't	Are you?
They are	They're	They are not	They aren't	Are they?

1 Write as in the example.

Long Form

1 It is   a doll.
2 They   dancers.
3 He   a teacher.
4 We   girls.
5 I   Tony.
6 She   a singer.

Short Form

It 's   a doll.
They   dancers.
He   a teacher.
We   girls.
I   Tony.
She   a singer.

The verb 'to be'

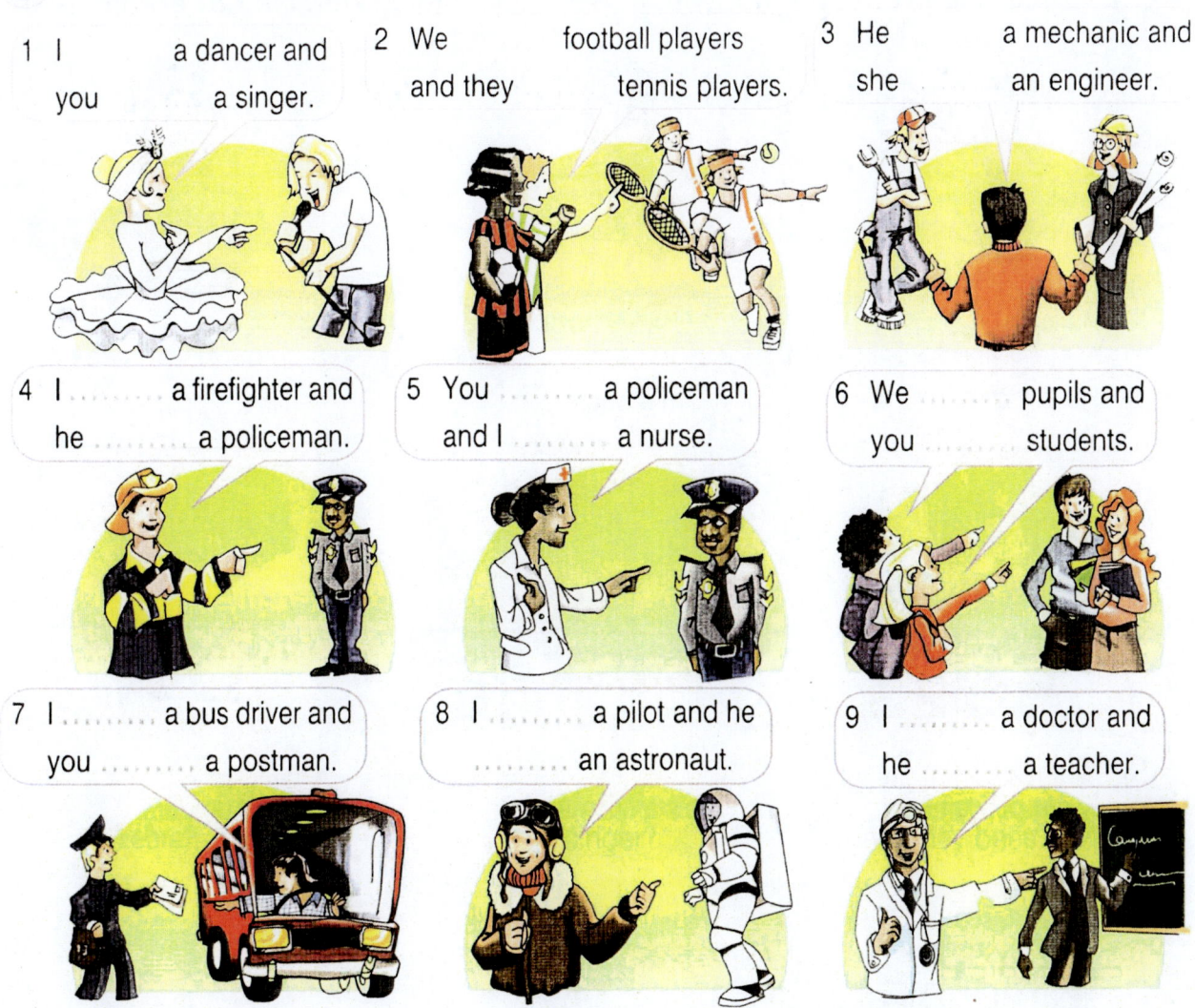

2 Fill in: *am*, *is* or *are*.

1 I ...... a dancer and you ...... a singer.
2 We ...... football players and they ...... tennis players.
3 He ...... a mechanic and she ...... an engineer.
4 I ...... a firefighter and he ...... a policeman.
5 You ...... a policeman and I ...... a nurse.
6 We ...... pupils and you ...... students.
7 I ...... a bus driver and you ...... a postman.
8 I ...... a pilot and he ...... an astronaut.
9 I ...... a doctor and he ...... a teacher.

3 Match column A with column B, then write the sentences.

A	B
1 I am a	A a box
2 He is	B Mary
3 It is	C Jim
4 She is	D pupil
5 We are	E singers

I am a pupil.

4 Fill in: *'m not*, *isn't* or *aren't*.

1 I *'m not* a teacher.
2 You ...... an engineer.
3 We ...... dancers.
4 He ...... a bus driver.
5 She ...... an astronaut.
6 I ...... a student.
7 They ...... postmen.
8 It ...... a dog.

The verb 'to be'

5 Fill in the pronoun *I*, *he*, *she*, *it*, *we*, *they* with *'m not*, *isn't* or *aren't*.

1 *He isn't* a policeman.   2 .... a teacher.   3 .... a postman.
He is a singer.   I'm a doctor.   He's a pilot.

4 .... firefighters.   5 .... an engineer.   6 .... singers.
They are policemen.   She's a teacher.   We are doctors.

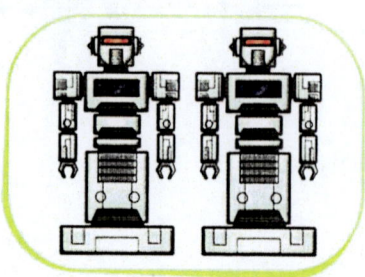  

7 .... balloons.   8 .... a fox.   9 .... a teacher.
They are robots.   It's a penguin.   She is a nurse.

6 Fill in: *Am*, *Is* or *Are*.

1 *Are* you a pupil?   5 .... you firefighters?
2 .... he a teacher?   6 .... it a dog?
3 .... they dancers?   7 .... she a nurse?
4 .... I a pilot?   8 .... it an apple?

The verb 'to be'

	Short answers	
Am I/Are you a pupil?	Yes, I am.	No, I'm not.
Is he/she/it big?	Yes, he/she/it is.	No, he/she/it isn't.
Are we/you/they pupils?	Yes, we/you/they are.	No, we/you/they aren't.

7 Answer the questions using short answers.

1 Is he 7?
No, he isn't.

2 Are they babies?

3 Is he a firefighter?

4 Is it a zebra?

5 Is she a singer?

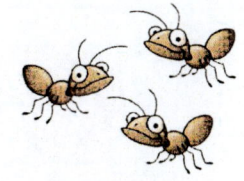
6 Are they bees?

8 Answer the questions.

1 Are they mechanics?
No, they aren't.
They're firefighters.

2 Is he a postman?

3 Is she a dancer?

4 Are you bus drivers?

5 Are they tennis players?

6 Is it a flower?

The verb 'to be'

9 Fill in: *am*, *is* or *are*. Listen and check.

I 1) .... Meena. I 2) .... 7. I 3) .... a pupil. Sunita 4) .... my mum. She 5) .... a teacher. Deepak 6) .... my dad. He 7) .... an engineer. Dev 8) .... my brother. He 9) .... a student. We 10) .... a happy family!

What am I?

Think of a job. Your partner asks three questions to guess who you are.

Are you a teacher?
Are you a bus driver?
Are you a pilot?

No, I'm not.
No, I'm not.
Yes, I am.

Writing Activity

Write a short text about you and your family. Use the text in Ex. 9 as a model.

Progress Check 3 (Units 5-6)

1 Match the words to the pictures.

1 I
2 he
3 she
4 it
5 we
6 they

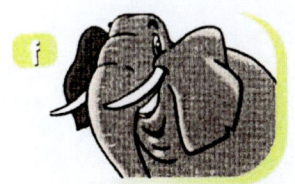

2 Read and circle.

1 I **am** / **are** five.
2 It **is** / **are** a bird.
3 We **am** / **are** Omar and Fatima.
4 She **is** / **are** a teacher.
5 I **is** / **am** Chris.
6 You **is** / **are** happy.

3 Write the sentences as in the example.

1 she / nurse   *She's a nurse.*
2 It / not apple
3 he / teacher?
4 They / not lions
5 I / student
6 She / Vera
7 it / elephant?
8 You / not doctor

4 Write the sentences as in the example.

1 Ann is a singer.
She is a singer.

2 Tom is a teacher.

3 Mark and Alice are dancers.

4 Spot and Dot are dogs.

5 Bob and I are firefighters.

6 Paul and Miko are pupils.

Progress Check 3

Listening

5 🎧29 Listen and tick (✓) the box. There is one example.

How old is Ellie?

A □   B ✓   C □

2 What's Mike's job?

A □   B □   C □

1 What is in the picture?

A □   B □   C □

3 Which is my dog?

A □ BARRY   B □ DASTY   C □ LARRY

6 🎧30 Song

She's a teacher
We are students
We're at school
We're at school
It's a sunny morning
We are very happy
School is cool
School is cool

It's an eraser
They are pencils
It's a book
It's a book
We are in the classroom
We are very happy
Come and look
Come and look

This / These – That / Those

🎧 **31** Listen and repeat.

This is a big egg.

These are crocodiles' eggs.

Look! *That* is a crocodile!

Those are crocodiles. Help!!

We use **this/these** for things near us.
We use **that/those** for things far from us.

This is a pen. **These** are pens.
That is a kite. **Those** are kites.

1 Look and complete the sentences. Use *This is* or *These are*.

1 .... These are .... hats.
2 .... skirt.
3 .... shirt.
4 .... dress.
5 .... trousers.
6 .... boots.

This / These – That / Those

2 Write sentences using **That** or **Those**.

1 .... That is a tiger. ....
2 ....
3 ....
4 ....
5 ....
6 ....

3 Fill in: **This** or **That**.

1 .... is a helicopter.

2 .... is a motorbike.

3 .... is a boat.

4 .... is a train.

This / These – That / Those

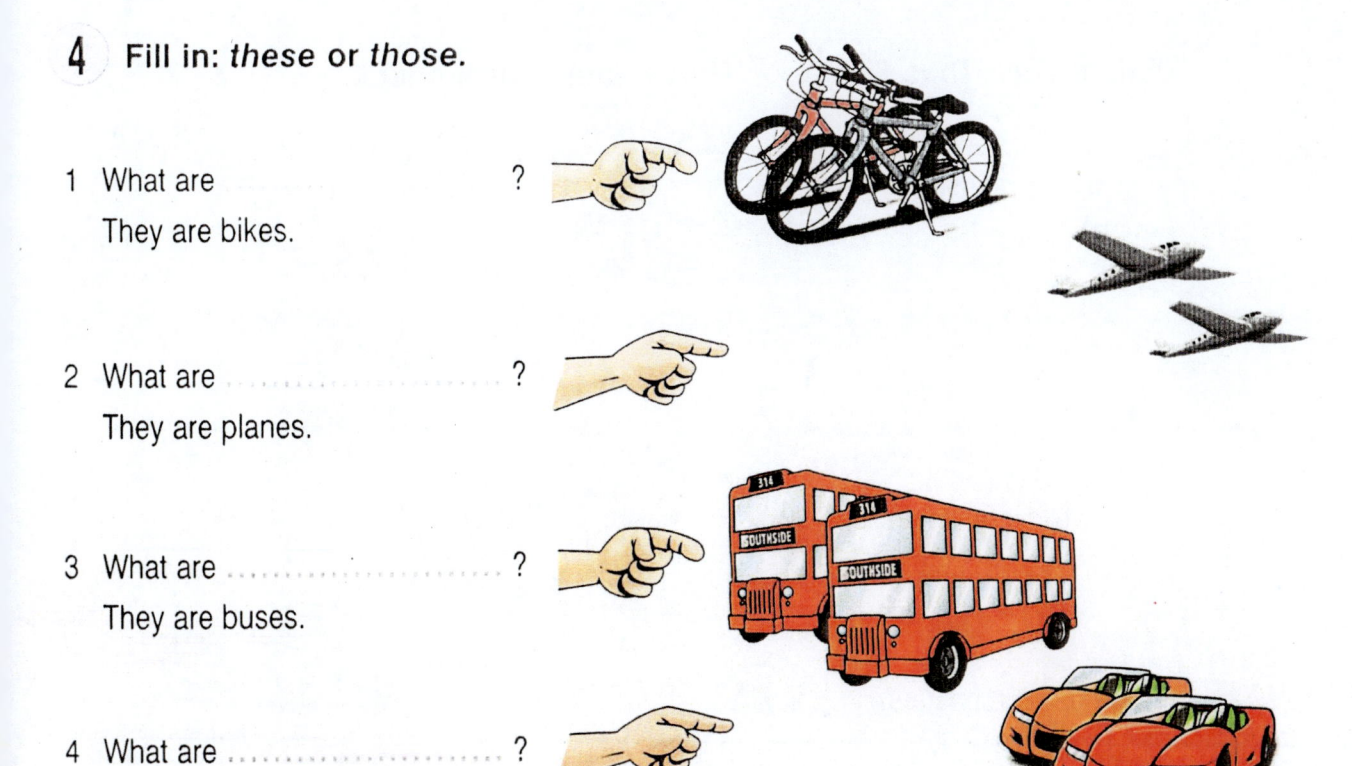

4 Fill in: *these* or *those*.

1 What are .... ?
  They are bikes.

2 What are .... ?
  They are planes.

3 What are .... ?
  They are buses.

4 What are .... ?
  They are cars.

5 Fill in: *this*, *that*, *these* or *those*.

1 What is .... ?
  It's a snake.

2 What are .... ?
  They're monkeys.

3 What is .... ?
  It's a bee.

4 What are .... ?
  They're shoes.

5 What is .... ?
  It's a cake.

6 What is .... ?
  It's my hat!!!

This / These – That / Those

6 🎧 32 Fill in: *This*, *That*, *These* or *Those*. Listen and check.

1 This .... is a blue monster.

2 .... is a red monster.

3 .... are yellow monsters.

4 .... are green monsters.

5 .... is a black monster.

6 .... is a white monster.

7 .... are brown monsters.

8 .... is a pink monster.

GAME — Say it right!

Student A: Point to things in the classroom. Make a wrong sentence.
Student B: Correct your partner.

This is a pen.

No, this isn't a pen. This is a pencil.

'Have / Have got'

🎧 33 Listen and repeat.

Have (got)

I've got a fish! What have you got?

Well, I haven't got a fish but I've got a boot.

Affirmative		Negative		Interrogative
Long form	Short Form	Long	Short Form	
I have got	I've got	I have not got	I haven't got	Have I got?
You have got	You've got	You have not got	You haven't got	Have you got?
He **has** got	He**'s** got	He **has not** got	He **hasn't** got	**Has** he got?
She **has** got	She**'s** got	She **has not** got	She **hasn't** got	**Has** she got?
It **has** got	It**'s** got	It **has not** got	It **hasn't** got	**Has** it got?
We have got	We've got	We have not got	We haven't got	Have we got?
You have got	You've got	You have not got	You haven't got	Have you got?
They have got	They've got	They have not got	They haven't got	Have they got?

1 Fill in the blanks as in the example.

Long form

1. I *have got* a book. (✓)
2. Mary .... a red dress. (✓)
3. They .... a dog. (✓)
4. It .... big ears. (✓)
5. Pam *has not got* a watch. (✗)
6. We .... a telephone. (✗)
7. Jane .... a banana. (✗)
8. You .... a hat. (✗)

Short form

I *'ve got* a book. (✓)
Mary .... a red dress. (✓)
They .... a dog. (✓)
It .... big ears. (✓)
Pam *hasn't got* a watch. (✗)
We .... a telephone. (✗)
Jane .... a banana. (✗)
You .... a hat. (✗)

B 'Have / Have got'

2 Look at the blue monster and write about it.

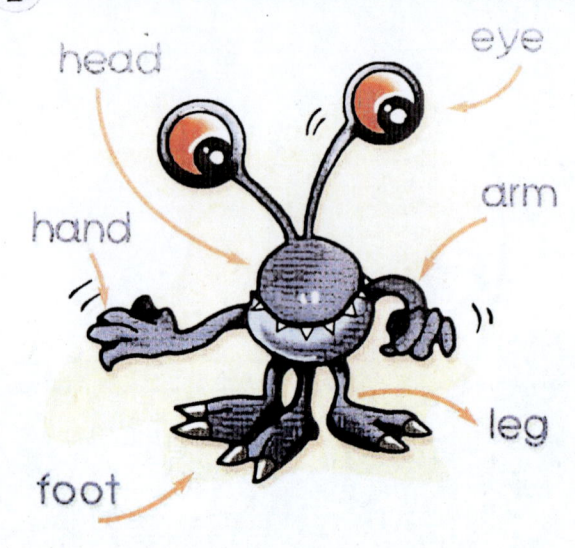

It has got two eyes.
....
....
....
....

3 Look at the pictures. Fill in: *'s got* or *hasn't got*.

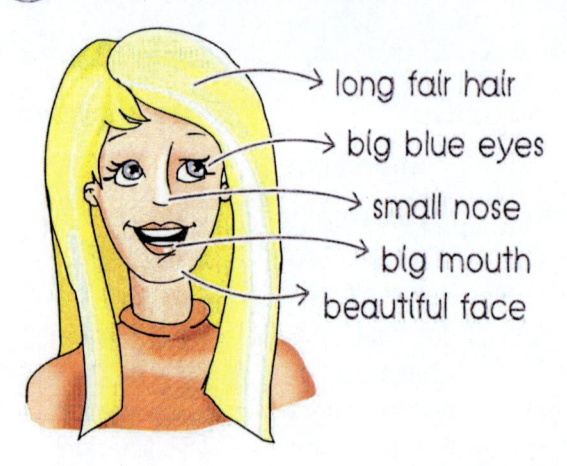

1 She **'s got** a beautiful face.
2 He .... big blue eyes.
3 She .... a big nose.
4 He .... big ears.
5 She .... a big mouth.
6 He .... a small nose.
7 She .... big ears.
8 He .... short brown hair.

4 Write the sentences in the negative.

1 We've got a big dog.
   We haven't got a big dog.
2 Omar's got a car.
   ....
3 Ben and Pat have got bikes.
   ....
4 Lucy's got a computer.
   ....
5 They've got a new house.
   ....
6 You've got a basketball.
   ....

'Have / Have got'

Short answers		
Have you got a pen?	Yes, I/we have.	No, I/we haven't.
Has he/she/it got two pens?	Yes, he/she/it has.	No, he/she/it hasn't.

5 Complete the sentences so that they are true about you and your friends/family.

1 I ...'ve got/haven't got... brown hair.
2 My dad .... a big nose.
3 My best friend .... a small mouth.
4 My teacher .... short fair hair.
5 I .... big ears.
6 My parents .... brown hair.
7 My mum .... long hair.
8 My friends .... bicycles.
9 I .... a kite.

6 Fill in: *Have* or *Has*. Write the short answers.

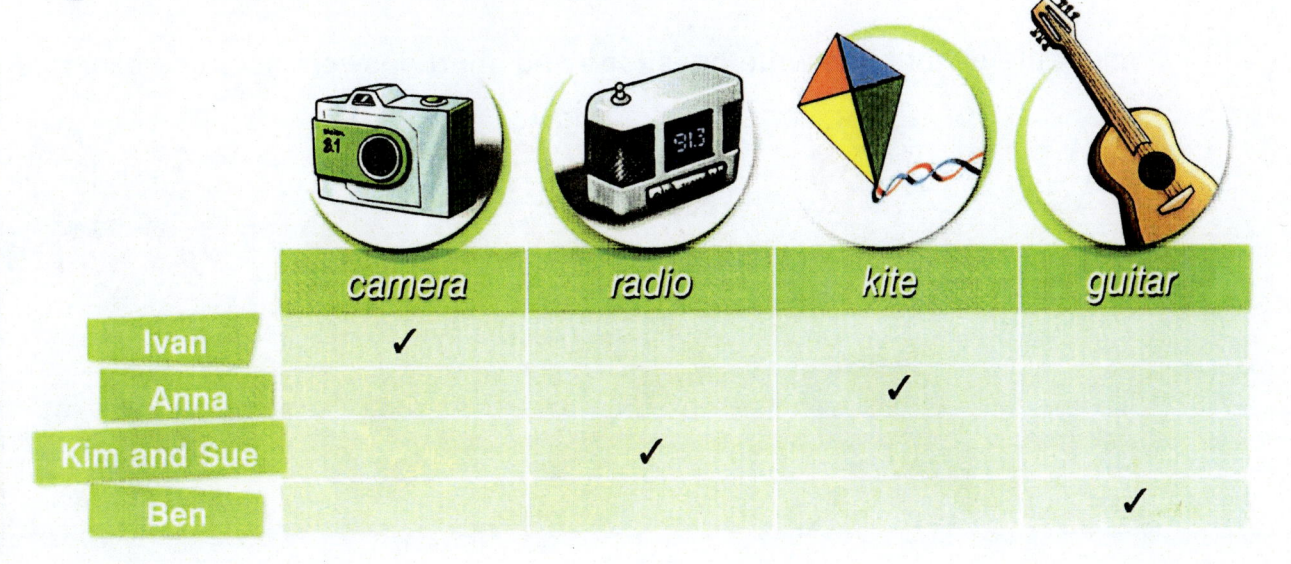

	camera	radio	kite	guitar
Ivan	✓			
Anna			✓	
Kim and Sue		✓		
Ben				✓

1 *Has* Ivan got a kite?
   No, he hasn't.
2 .... Anna got a kite?
3 .... Kim and Sue got a radio?
4 .... Ben got a camera?
5 .... Kim and Sue got a kite?
6 .... Ben got a guitar?
7 .... Anna got a radio?
8 .... Ivan got a camera?

'Have / Have got'

7 Write questions and short answers as in the example.

1 it/big ears
   Has it got big ears?
   Yes, it has.

2 she/cat

3 they/horse

4 we/hats

5 she/guitar

6 he/motorbike

8 Look at the picture and write questions and short answers as in the example.

1 Alex/umbrella
   Has Alex got an umbrella?
   No, he hasn't.

2 Mr and Mrs Olsen/dog

3 Olga/toy robot

4 Anya/ball

5 Hanna and Otto/guitar

6 Anya/umbrella

'Have / Have got'

What have they got?

Look at the pictures for a minute. Say what you remember.

A B

JANE TOM BEN ANDY

Team A S1: Jane has got a dog in Picture A. In picture B she hasn't got a dog. She's got a cat.

Speaking Activity

Describe a boy or a girl from the class. Your partner guesses who it is.

This person has got short fair hair, a small nose and blue eyes.

Is it Elena?

Yes, it is.

Writing Activity

Describe your best friend.

Stick a photo here.

.... has got ....
.... hair and .... eyes.
.... nose.
.... mouth and
.... ears. .... face.

41

Progress Check 4 (Units 7-8)

1 Read and circle.

1 This / **Those** are birds.
2 That / These are hats. 
3 That / These is a dolphin. 
4 These / Those are lemons. 
5 This / That is a TV. 
6 Those / This is a kite. 
7 These / That are erasers. 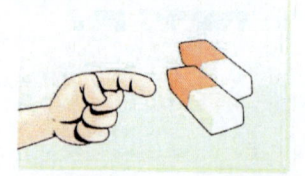
8 Those / That is an elephant. 

2 Fill in: *this*, *that*, *these* or *those*.

1 *This* is  a banana and .... is .... an apple.
2 .... are .... oranges and .... are .... lemons.
3 .... is .... a pineapple and .... are .... strawberries.

3 Write the questions and answer them as in the example.

1 *Has he got a ball?* (he/ball/✓)
   Yes, he has.
2 .... (she/toy robot/✗)
3 .... (we/yo-yo/✗)
4 .... (you/umbrella/✗)
5 .... (they/books/✓)
6 .... (he/schoolbag/✓)

42

Progress Check 4

4 Write the negative or affirmative sentences.

1. We have got a horse.
   We haven't got a horse.

2. Jane hasn't got a monkey.

3. Yasmin has got five cats.

4. Heath and Jake haven't got a mouse.

5. You haven't got a snake.

6. Kate and Leo have got two fish.

Listening

5 🎧 34 Listen and draw lines. There is one example.

Mark   Jill   Dave   Paul   Helen   Ben   Sarah

6 🎧 35 Song

These are my boots and that's my hat
I've got clothes, I've got clothes
Those are my trousers, that's my shirt
I can go outside to play

This is my ball and that's my kite
I've got toys, I've got toys
Those are my yo-yos, that's my bike
I can go outside to play

There is / There are

🎧 36 **Listen and repeat.**

There is a boat.
There are three fish.
There isn't an octopus.
There aren't four starfish.

	Affirmative		Negative		Interrogative
	Long Form	Short Form	Long Form	Short Form	
singular	there is	there's	there is not	there isn't	Is there?
plural	there are		there are not	there aren't	Are there?

1 Look at the picture. Read and write *yes* or *no*.

1 There are two children in the picture. — Yes
2 There are four bikes.
3 There isn't a dog.
4 There are five bananas.
5 There is a radio.
6 There are two sandwiches.

There is / There are

2 Look at the picture. Fill in: *is*, *are*, *isn't*, *aren't*. Listen and check.

1 There .... a helicopter.
2 There .... three cars.
3 There .... a park.
4 There .... a house.
5 There .... three children in the park.
6 There .... a lorry.
7 There .... a supermarket.
8 There .... three lorries.

3 Look at the picture. Read and tick (✓).

1 Are there five children in the picture?
   a Yes, there are.   ☐
   b No, there aren't. ✓

2 Is there a snake?
   a Yes, there are. ☐
   b Yes, there is.   ☐

3 Are there three frogs?
   a Yes, there are.   ☐
   b No, there aren't. ☐

4 Are there two dogs?
   a No, there isn't. ☐
   b No, there aren't. ☐

5 Is there a cat?
   a No, there aren't. ☐
   b No, there isn't. ☐

6 Is there a dolphin?
   a No, there isn't. ☐
   b No, there aren't. ☐

There is / There are

6 Look at the picture. Write questions and answers as in the example.

1 hat
   Is there a hat?
   Yes, there is.

2 three books
   Are there three books?
   No, there aren't.

3 doll
   ....
   ....

4 four red dresses
   ....
   ....

5 umbrella
   ....
   ....

GAME — Where am I?

Think of a room. Your partner asks you three questions and tries to guess where you are.

- Is there a sofa? — No, there isn't.
- Are there cupboards? — Yes, there are.
- Are you in the kitchen? — Yes, I am!

Writing Activity

Write what there is in your bedroom.

In my bedroom, there is ...

'Can'

Listen and repeat.

I can walk and
I can talk.
I can't fly and
I can't cry.
Can you sing
and can you dance?
I can clap my hands!!!

Affirmative	Negative		Interrogative
	Long Form	Short Form	
I can	I cannot	I can't	Can I?
You can	You cannot	You can't	Can you?
He can	He cannot	He can't	Can he?
She can	She cannot	She can't	Can she?
It can	It cannot	It can't	Can it?
We can	We cannot	We can't	Can we?
You can	You cannot	You can't	Can you?
They can	They cannot	They can't	Can they?

Short answers	Can you dance?	Yes, I can./No, I can't.

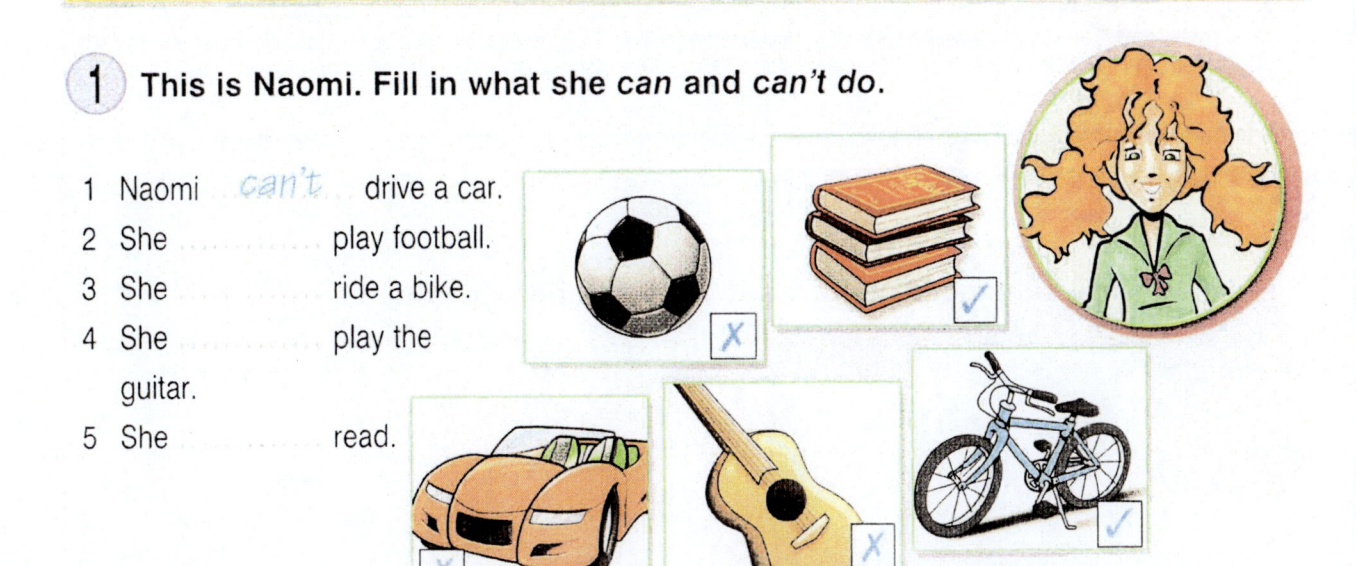

1 This is Naomi. Fill in what she *can* and *can't do*.

1 Naomi _can't_ drive a car.
2 She .... play football.
3 She .... ride a bike.
4 She .... play the guitar.
5 She .... read.

'Can'

2 Look at the pictures. Tick (✓) what you can do and cross (✗) what you can't do.

1 dance ☐   2 sing ☐   3 swim ☐   4 drive ☐

5 ride a horse ☐   6 write ☐   7 run fast ☐   8 climb ☐

9 ride a bike ☐   10 cook ☐   11 play tennis ☐   12 paint ☐

● Now write sentences about what you can and can't do.

1   I can't drive.   5
2   6
3   7
4   8

49

'Can'

3 First say then write sentences as in the example.

1 Can you see a truck?
2 Can you see a man?
3 Can you see a bed?
4 Can you see a boy?
5 Can you see a dog?
6 Can you see a glass?

4 Look at the pictures and read the answers. Then write the questions.

Jonas

Kim and Ben

Stella

1 *Can Jonas play the guitar*? Yes, he can.

2 ....? No, they can't.

3 ....? Yes, she can.

Antonio

Pat and Tina

Alina

4 ....? No, he can't.

5 ....? Yes, they can.

6 ....? No, she can't.

5 🎧 39 Write out the questions and answers with *can/can't*. Listen and check.

1 dogs / fly
   Can dogs fly?
   No, they can't.

2 frogs / jump

3 snakes / walk

4 monkeys / climb

6 Look at the picture. Use the phrases below to write questions and answers as in the example.

play basketball   read   climb a tree   play football   fly a kite   ride a bike

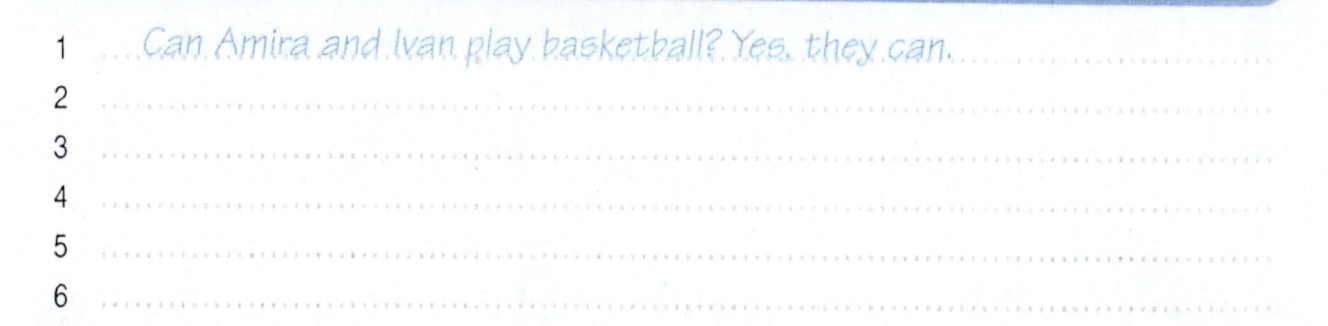

1 Can Amira and Ivan play basketball? Yes, they can.
2
3
4
5
6

7 True or False?

1 Fish can swim.
   True! Fish can swim.

2 Dogs can read.

3 Dolphins can walk.

4 Spiders can swim.

5 Kangaroos can jump.

6 Chickens can fly.

'Can'

Guess the Animal!

Think of an animal. Your partner asks you questions with *can* and tries to guess the animal.

Can it jump? — Yes, it can.
Can it fly? — No, it can't.
Can it swim? — Yes, it can.
Is it a frog? — Yes, it is!

Speaking Activity

Look at the table. In pairs ask and answer questions about what the people *can* and *can't do*.

	Tony	Céline	Chloe & Phil
play tennis	✓	✗	✓
paint	✗	✓	✓
dance	✗	✓	✓
swim	✓	✗	✗

Can Tony play tennis? — Yes, he can.

Writing Activity

Ask a friend and write down four things he or she can do and four things he or she can't do.

Progress Check 5 (Units 9–10)

1 Complete the sentences with *There is*, *There are*, *There isn't* or *There aren't*.

1 There is   a computer.
2 ....   four flowers.
3 ....   two glasses.
4 ....   a picture.
5 ....   four books.
6 ....   an eraser.
7 ....   a schoolbag.
8 ....   two pens.

2 Look at the picture and answer the questions.

1 Is there a rabbit in the picture?   Yes, there is.
2 Is there a dog in the picture?   ....
3 Are there birds in the picture?   ....
4 Is there a girl in the picture?   ....
5 Are there houses in the picture?   ....
6 Are there trees in the picture?   ....

3 Look at the table. Write what Chelsea *can* or *can't* do.

Chelsea	Yes	No
play the guitar	✓	
ride a bike	✓	
sing		✓
play tennis	✓	
drive a car		✓
swim		✓

1 She can play the guitar.
2 ....
3 ....
4 ....
5 ....
6 ....

Progress Check 5

4 Write questions and answers. Use *can* or *can't*.

1 Mimi / swim? (✗)   *Can Mimi swim? No, she can't.*
2 Jane and Ted / cook? (✗)
3 the cat / run fast? (✓)
4 he / eat that cake? (✗)
5 your friends / play football? (✓)
6 she / ride a bike? (✓)

Listening

5 🎧 40 Listen and write a name or a number. There are two examples.

Charles — *12* — 1

2 .... 3 .... 4 ....

6 🎧 41 Song

There are lions in the zoo
And they can walk
There's a parrot in the zoo
And it can talk
There are lots of things to see
Please come to the zoo with me
There's a parrot in the zoo
And it can talk

There's a dolphin in the zoo
And it can swim
There are lots of pretty birds
And they can sing
There are lots of things to do
Can we all go to the zoo
There's a dolphin in the zoo
And it can swim

Possessives

Listen and repeat.

Possessives

"That's my car!"

"Yes, that's your car and this is your ticket."

Personal Pronouns		Possessive adjectives	
Singular	Plural	Singular	Plural
I	we	my	our
you	you	your	your
he, she, it	they	his, her, its	their

1 Fill in: *my*, *your*, *his*, *her*, *its*, *our* or *their*.

1 I've got a scarf.
   It's ....my.... scarf.

2 He's got a jacket.
   It's .... jacket.

3 She's got a hat.
   It's .... hat.

4 They've got glasses.
   They're .... glasses.

5 You've got a handbag.
   It's .... handbag.

6 We've got dresses.
   They're .... dresses.

7 It's got a house.
   It's .... house.

8 They've got T-shirts.
   They're .... T-shirts.

9 I've got a blue top.
   It's .... top.

55

Possessives

2 Fill in: *my*, *your*, *his*, *her*, *its*, *our* or *their*.

1 This is Alejandro and this is *his* dog.
2 This is Marcie and this is .... computer. 
3 This is Enzo and Lea and this is .... cat. 
4 This is me and this is .... bike. 
5 This is you and this is .... parrot. 
6 We are Vadim and Taras and this is .... snake. 
7 This is a dog and this is .... house. 
8 This is me and this is .... kite. 
9 This is Sanne and Anouk and this is .... rabbit. 

3 Fill in: *my*, *your*, *his*, *her*, *its*, *our* or *their*.

1 I have got a house. It's *my* house.
2 Ali and Hamid have got watches. They're .... watches.
3 My friends and I have got a ball. It's .... ball.
4 Tito has got a bike. It's .... bike.
5 My mum has got a dress. It's .... dress.
6 My cat has got a bed. It's .... bed.
7 You've got a car. It's .... car.

4 🎧 43 Fill in: *my*, *his*, *her*, *its*, *our* or *their*. Listen and check.

1 A: Have Cho and Eri got a robot?
   B: Yes, it's *their* robot.
2 A: Look, he's got a dog.
   B: Yes, it's .... dog.
3 A: Is this Anna's doll?
   B: Yes, it's .... doll.
4 A: Look, the dog has got a ball.
   B: Yes, it's .... ball.
5 A: Has your family got a TV?
   B: Yes, it's .... TV.
6 A: Is this your house?
   B: Yes. It's .... house.

Possessives

Possessive case

We use **'s** with one person or animal.

Diego's book

the girl's cat

We use **s'** with more than one person or animal.

the boys' books   BUT   the children's dog

NOTE:

Ben and Joe's bike

Ben's and Joe's bikes

5 Add 's or '. Write the words.

~~the dog~~   ~~our cats~~   the lion   my dad   the rabbits   my teacher
our friends   your sister   my brothers   the monkeys

's

the dog's

'

our cats'

Possessives

6 Read and circle.

1 They're the **girls** / **girls'** dolls.
2 She's **Sarahs'** / **Sarah's** mum.
3 He's my **dad's** / **dad** brother.
4 They are the **boy's** / **boys** trains.
5 It's the **mouses** / **mouse's** house.
6 It's **Christina's** / **Christinas'** T-shirt.
7 She's **Karim and Hasem's** / **Karim's and Hasem's** sister.
8 They're **Alphonso's and Fernando** / **Alphonso's and Fernando's** dogs

7 Match the phrases to the pictures.

1 2 3 4

A the boy's bike
B the girl's brush
C the girls' brushes
D the boys' bikes

8 Look and write.

🎧 44 Listen and check.

1 Sandra is ....*Jenny*.... and ....*Harry's*.... mum.
2 David is .... and .... grandpa.
3 Cassie is .... and .... grandma.
4 Jenny is .... sister.
5 Harry is .... brother.
6 William is .... and .... dad.

Possessives

Speaking Activity

Look at the family on page 58. Ask questions.

Who's David?

David is Jenny's grandpa. He is William's dad.

GAME

Who's this?

Write 5 names of people in your family. Ask and answer questions.

1 ....Elsie............
2 ....
3 ....
4 ....
5 ....

Is Elsie your sister?

Is Elsie your grandma?

No, she isn't.

Yes, she is!

Writing Activity

Write about your family.

...My name is........

The Imperative

🎧 45 **Listen and repeat.**

"Look at my hat! Isn't it pretty?"

"That is my hat! Don't wear it!"

We use the **imperative** to tell one or more people to do or not to do something.

1 🎧 46 **Write. Listen and check.**

~~Answer~~   Write   Sit   Read   Listen   Colour

1. ..Answer.. the question.
2. .... the picture.
3. .... down.
4. .... to this song.
5. .... your name in capital letters.
6. .... the sign!

The Imperative

Positive — Open the window, please!

Negative — Don't open the door!

2 Write the negative form.

1 Close your book!
   Don't close your book!

2 Wear your jacket!

3 Run!

4 Look at me!

3 Match the sentences to the pictures.

Don't talk!
Look at the board!
Don't take photos!
Don't eat in here!
Don't sit there!

4 Put the words in order.

1 hair / brush / your.

2 the / music / listen to.

3 picture / look at / the.

4 down / jump / and / up!

5 to / count / 10.

6 cola / don't / drink.

7 sing / in class / don't.

8 your / dinner / eat .

The Imperative

5 🎧 Match the sentences with the pictures. Listen and check.

Brush your teeth!   Tidy your room!   Do your homework!
Go to bed!   Drink your milk! Wake up!

1 Wake up!
2
3
4
5
6

6 Tick then write.

In the classroom ...	Do	Don't
Eat.		✓
Be quiet.		
Play football.		
Listen to your teacher.		
Look at the board.		
Look out the window.		

1 .... Don't eat! ....
2 ....
3 ....
4 ....
5 ....
6 ....

GAME — Don't do that!

Tell your partner to do the opposite.

Don't jump!

(jumping)

Progress Check 6 (Units 11-12)

1 Look at the pictures. Rewrite the sentences. Change the underlined words. Use *your*, *his*, *her*, *their* or *our*.

1 This is Claudia's dress.
   This is her dress.

2 That's Mr and Mrs Smith's car.

3 These aren't Marco's toys.

4 This is Greg's and my house.

5 This isn't Sarah's hat.

6 Those are your and your sister's schoolbags.

2 Match the sentences to the pictures.

Eat your lunch, please.   Go to sleep.   Brush your teeth!
Climb that tree!   Don't talk!   Don't run!

1 Eat your lunch, please.
2 
3 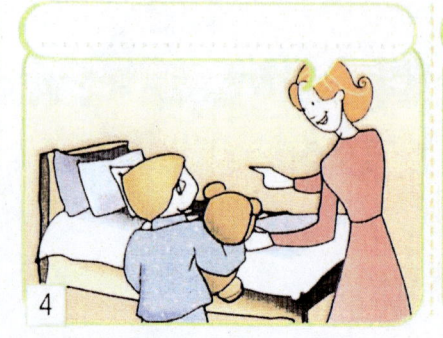
4 
5 
6

Progress Check 6

3 Fill in 's or '.

1 Those are Ralph ____ shoes.
2 This is Carla ____ umbrella.
3 They are the boys ____ bikes.
4 This is the children ____ computer.
5 Those are the women ____ watches.
6 This is Charlie ____ bag.
7 Those are the monkeys ____ bananas.
8 It's the baby ____ toy.

Listening

4 🎧 48 Listen and colour. There is one example.

Song

5 🎧 49

Jump up and down with me
Jump up and down with me
Sing our song and clap your hands
Jump up and down with me

Stand up, sit down with me
Stand up, sit down with me
We can sing our happy song
Stand up, sit down with me

Present Continuous

Present Continuous

🎧 50 Listen and repeat.

Two frogs are standing by,
Two butterflies are flying high,
and to the frogs they're saying goodbye.
He's singing, she's dancing,
they're running, they're jumping,
they're playing in the sun,
they're having fun.

Affirmative		Negative	
Long form	Short Form	Long form	Short Form
I am walking	I'm walking	I am not walking	I'm not walking
You are walking	You're walking	You are not walking	You aren't walking
He is walking	He's walking	He is not walking	He isn't walking
She is walking	She's walking	She is not walking	She isn't walking
It is walking	It's walking	It is not walking	It isn't walking
We are walking	We're walking	We are not walking	We aren't walking
You are walking	You're walking	You are not walking	You aren't walking
They are walking	They're walking	They are not walking	They aren't walking

Spelling rules

work – working, read – reading, climb – climbing, fly – flying
BUT: cut – cutting, put – putting, write – writing, dance – dancing

We use the present continuous for actions happening now. He is sleeping now.

1 Add *-ing* to the verbs.

1 climb   *climbing*
2 swim
3 cut
4 cook
5 ride
6 run
7 dance
8 write
9 say

Present Continuous

2 Fill in: *am*, *is* or *are*.

1 He .... eating a banana.
2 It .... flying.
3 I .... reading.
4 They .... dancing.
5 We .... walking.
6 She .... cooking.

3 Complete the sentences as in the example.

--- Long form ---

1 I ...am... singing. (✓)
2 We .... brushing our teeth. (✓)
3 He .... doing his homework. (✓)
4 It .... flying. (✓)
5 They ...are not... drinking tea. (✗)
6 You .... sitting. (✗)
7 She .... swimming. (✗)
8 It .... barking. (✗)

--- Short form ---

I 'm singing. (✓)
We .... brushing our teeth. (✓)
He .... doing his homework. (✓)
It .... flying. (✓)
They ...aren't... drinking tea. (✗)
You .... sitting. (✗)
She .... swimming. (✗)
It .... barking. (✗)

4 Look at the picture and use the verbs in brackets to complete the sentences.

1 ...Bea and Tony are making... (make) a sandcastle.
2 .... (wear) red T-shirts.
3 .... (eat) an ice cream.
4 .... (sit) under a beach umbrella.
5 .... (swim).
6 .... (write) her name on the sand.

Present Continuous

5 Fill in: *'m not*, *aren't* or *isn't*.

1 Carmen .... eating a banana.
2 Angelo .... talking to Fabio.
3 You .... listening to the radio.
4 They .... playing tennis.
5 It .... running fast.
6 I .... going to school.

6 Look at the pictures and use the verbs below to write what the people are doing as in the example.

drive   swim   sit   play   eat   read

1 Maria is drinking milk.
Maria isn't drinking milk.
She's eating an apple.

2 Ivan and Katya are dancing.

3 Billy is making a sandcastle.

4 Paolo is riding a motorbike.

5 Susan and Miriam are listening to music.

6 Joshua is painting a picture.

Present Continuous

Is it raining outside?

No, it isn't. It's snowing!

Listen and repeat.

Interrogative

Am I walking?
Are you walking?
Is he walking?
Is she walking?
Is it walking?
Are we walking?
Are you walking?
Are they walking?

Short answers

Are you/we/they reading?	Yes, I am/we/they are.	Is he/she/it reading?	Yes, he/she/it is.
	No, I'm not/we/they aren't.		No, he/she/it isn't.

7 Answer the questions. Use short answers.

1 Is the man painting?
   Yes, he is.

2 Are the women eating?

3 Is Joe riding a bike?

4 Is Li taking a photo?

5 Is Sarah sleeping?

6 Are Maya and Eve swimming?

Present Continuous

8 Write the questions. Answer them.

1 Mum / cook? (✗)
2 the dogs / sleep? (✓)
3 your sister / write a letter? (✗)
4 Chris / sit in the garden? (✓)
5 you / talk on the phone? (✗)

9 Put the verbs in brackets into the *present continuous*.

Dear Lena,
We are in Amalfi, Italy. I 1) .... (sit) on the beach and I 2) .... (listen) to music. Mum and Dad 3) .... (swim). My sister 4) .... (eat) an ice cream and my brother 5) .... (make) a sandcastle. It's fantastic here!
Love,
Darya

GAME — What are you doing?

Mime an action. Your partner guesses what you are doing.

- Are you riding a bicycle?
- Are you driving a car?
- No, I'm not.
- Yes, I am!

Writing Activity

You are on holiday. Write a postcard.

Dear ....,
We are in .... I ....
.... Mum and Dad ....
....
Love,

Present Simple

Listen and repeat. 🎧 52

*Do and does, does and do
This is what I usually do
I fish with my net
I feed my little pet
I swim and run
my life is fun.*

Present Simple

Affirmative	Negative	
	Long form	Short Form
I walk	I do not walk	I don't walk
You walk	You do not walk	You don't walk
He walks	He does not walk	He doesn't walk
She walks	She does not walk	She doesn't walk
It walks	It does not walk	It doesn't walk
We walk	We do not walk	We don't walk
You walk	You do not walk	You don't walk
They walk	They do not walk	They don't walk

We use the present simple for repeated actions or permanent situations.

Spelling of 3rd person singular for verbs ending in:

ss, sh, ch, x, o + es	consonant + y → ies	vowel + y + s
I brush - he brushes	I cry - he cries	I play - he plays

1 Write the third person singular.

1 I swim – it *swims*
2 I try – she
3 I enjoy – he
4 I fly – it
5 I run – she
6 I catch – he
7 I like – he
8 I push – she
9 I say – it

Present Simple

2 🎧 53 Write the verbs in the correct columns. Listen and check. Listen and repeat.

wash   write   surf   read   ~~stop~~   wear   close   look
~~watch~~   play   mix   sleep   kiss   ~~do~~   open

/s/ /f/, /k/, /p/, /t/	/iz/ /s/, /ʃ/, /tʃ/, /z/, /dʒ/	/z/ after other sounds
stops,	watches,	does,

3 Complete the sentences as in the example.

Long Form
1. We ......do not...... like football.
2. He .... eat fish.
3. She .... watch TV.
4. I .... drive a car.
5. They .... play tennis.
6. Kate .... speak French.
7. You .... get up at 7:00.

Short Form
We ......don't...... like football.
He .... eat fish.
She .... watch TV.
I .... drive a car.
They .... play tennis.
Kate .... speak French.
You .... get up at 7:00.

4 Look at the table and write what sports they *play* and *don't play*.

	football	tennis	basketball
Phil	✓	✓	
Sofia & Chris		✓	✓
Rose	✓		✓
Zack		✓	✓
Anna & I	✓	✓	

1. Phil plays football and tennis. He doesn't play basketball.
2. ....
3. ....
4. ....
5. ....

Present Simple

5 Write what Carol does every day.

Carol 1) *gets up* at 7 o'clock every day. She 2) _____ breakfast at 7:30. She 3) _____ to school at 8 o'clock. She 4) _____ lunch at 2 o'clock. She 5) _____ her homework in the evening. She 6) _____ TV at 8 o'clock. She 7) _____ to bed at 10 o'clock.

get up
have breakfast
go to bed
go to school
watch TV
do homework
have lunch

6 Use the words to write sentences. Use the *present simple*.

1 do their shopping / every Friday / they

They do their shopping every Friday.

2 ride her bike / she / every day

3 at 7:30 / dinner / eat / they

4 often play / my dad and I / football

5 his homework / he do / in the afternoon

6 a pilot / planes / fly

Present Simple

Interrogative	Short Answers
Do I walk?	Yes, I **do**. / No, I **don't**.
Do you walk?	Yes, you **do**. / No, you **don't**.
Does he walk?	Yes, he **does**. / No, he **doesn't**.
Does she walk?	Yes, she **does**. / No, she **doesn't**.
Does it walk?	Yes, it **does**. / No, it **doesn't**.
Do we walk?	Yes, we **do**. / No, we **don't**.
Do you walk?	Yes, you **do**. / No, you **don't**.
Do they walk?	Yes, they **do**. / No, they **don't**.

Do you know six animals from Africa?

Yes, I do. Two tigers and four monkeys!

7 Fill in: *Do* or *Does*.

1 ...Do... you speak English?
2 .... your mum bring you to school?
3 .... you like your new school?
4 .... you play basketball?
5 .... your friend come to this school?
6 .... your dad drive?

8 Write the questions.

1 like / you / chocolate — *Do you like chocolate?*
2 she / the guitar / play
3 listen to / Carlos / music
4 dogs / run fast
5 English / speak / your friend
6 Liz and Ben / school / go to

Present Simple

9 Complete the questions and answers.

1	Do	you	like	strawberries? (like)	Yes, I do.
2		Candice and Alfonso		to school? (walk)	No,
3		Mary		TV in the afternoon? (watch)	Yes,
4		they		basketball on Saturdays? (play)	No,
5		Chris		meat every day? (eat)	No,
6		Mr Key		in the sea? (swim)	Yes,

10 Fill in: *Do* or *Does*. Answer the questions.

1 .... you and your friends walk to school?
2 .... your best friend play football?
3 .... you go to the beach on Sundays?
4 .... you and your friends play computer games?
5 .... your teacher ride a motorbike?

11 Put the verbs in brackets into the *present simple*, then answer the questions as in the example.

John and David are friends. They 1) *like* (like) sports and they 2) .... (play) basketball every week. They 3) .... (not/play) tennis. David 4) .... (like) running. John 5) .... (like) reading books. Every night he 6) .... (read) a story before he 7) .... (go) to bed.

1 Do John and David like sports?   Yes, they do.
2 Do John and David play basketball?
3 Do John and David play tennis?
4 Does David like running?
5 Does John like reading books?
6 Does John read stories every night?

Present Simple

What do you do at …?

Say a time. Your partner mimes what he/she usually does at that time. Tell the class.

What do you do at 7 o'clock in the morning?

Peter brushes his teeth at 7 o'clock in the morning.

Present Simple vs Present Continuous

We use the **present simple** for repeated actions or permanent situations.
Phrases with the Present Simple: *usually, always, often, never, every day,* etc.

We use the **present continuous** for temporary actions or actions happening now.
Phrases with the present continuous: *now, at present, today, at the moment,* etc.

Usually
He **usually** drives a car.

Today
Today he is riding a bike.

12 Put the verbs in brackets into the *present simple* or the *present continuous*.

1 **(drink)**
I usually ....*drink*........ tea. Today I ....*'m drinking*........ coffee.

2 **(eat)**
He usually .... lunch at one o'clock. Today he .... lunch at 2:00.

3 **(read)**
She .... now. She often .... in the evening.

4 **(wash)**
Lewis .... the car at the moment. He usually .... it every Saturday.

5 **(ride)**
Maria .... her bike every day. She .... her bike now.

6 **(wear)**
James and Mike usually .... jackets but today they .... T-shirts.

Present Simple

13 Fill in the verbs in the *present simple* or the *present continuous*.

listen   watch   cook   swim   read   play   run   eat

1 Roger usually *listens* to music but today he *is playing* the guitar.

2 They usually .... dinner but today they .... pizza.

3 Jennifer usually .... TV but today she .... a book.

4 He usually .... but today he ....

14 Put the verbs in brackets into the *present simple* or the *present continuous*.

usually

today

Olivia usually 1) *wears* (wear) T-shirts. In the afternoon, she usually 2) .... (go) to the park and she 3) .... (walk) her dog. She often 4) .... (play) football in the park at the weekend. She usually 5) .... (eat) apples and oranges for a snack. Today, Olivia is at a party. She 6) .... (wear) a beautiful dress. She 7) .... (talk) to her friends now. She 8) .... (eat) an ice cream. Olivia and her friends 9) .... (listen) to music. They 10) .... (have) fun!

Present Simple

15 Put the verbs in brackets into the *present simple* or the *present continuous*.

1 I _play_ (play) tennis every week.
2 The children _____ (eat) lunch now.
3 _____ Marla _____ (clean) her bedroom every Saturday?
4 We _____ (not/watch) TV at the moment.
5 He _____ (go) to school every day.
6 I _____ (read) a book now.
7 They _____ (not/ride) their bikes now.
8 _____ she _____ (listen) to music at the moment?

16 Put the verbs in brackets into the *present simple* or the *present continuous*.

To: yannisfun@gomail.com
From: simon_10@happymail.uk
Subject: Holiday Time!

Dear Yann,
I 1) _am_ (be) on holiday with my family. We 2) _____ (be) in Nice, France. We 3) _____ (stay) in a great hotel by the sea. In the mornings, we usually 4) _____ (go) to the beach and we 5) _____ (swim) in the sea. In the evenings, we 6) _____ (eat) at nice restaurants. At the moment, Mum and Dad 7) _____ (walk) on the beach and my sister 8) _____ (take) photos. I 9) _____ (sit) in our hotel room and I 10) _____ (write) emails to all my friends. France is great!
See you soon,
Simon

17 🎧 54 Put the verbs in brackets into the *present simple* or the *present continuous*. Listen and check.

Claude: Hi Stella. What 1) _are you doing_ (you/do)?
Stella: I 2) _____ (read) a book about Australia. It's really good.
Claude: 3) _____ (you/read) a lot of books?
Stella: Yes, lots! 4) _____ (meet) Jake today?
Claude: Yes, we 5) _____ (ride) our bikes to the sports field because we 6) _____ (play) football this afternoon.
Stella: 7) _____ (you/play) football every Saturday?
Claude: No, we usually 8) _____ (go) to the swimming pool on Saturdays.

Present Simple

Speaking Activity

Look at the pictures. Ask and answers questions with your partner.

Usually (6 o'clock in the evening)   Now (6 o'clock in the evening)

Mr Jones
Mrs Jones
Ann
Ben and Sue

What does Ann usually do at 6 o'clock in the evening?

She usually reads a book.

It's 6 o'clock in the evening. What is she doing now?

She is watching TV.

Writing Activity

Imagine you are on holiday. Write an email to your friend. Write about your holiday. What do you usually do? What are you and your family doing at the moment?

To: my_friend@gomail.com
From: me@happymail.uk
Subject: Holiday Time!

Dear _____,
I am on holiday ....
....
....
....

See you soon,

Progress Check 7 (Units 13-14)

1 Match the sentences.

1. [E] Are you doing your homework?
2. [ ] Is she drinking milk?
3. [ ] Is it climbing a tree?
4. [ ] Are they reading books?
5. [ ] Are we playing football?

A No, it isn't.
B No, we aren't.
C Yes, she is.
D Yes, they are.
E Yes, I am.

2 Fill in the correct form of the verbs. Then match the sentences to the pictures.

draw   go   watch   swim   play   eat

1. [C] Dana ...goes... dancing on Thursdays.
2. [ ] My brother and I .... football in the park now.
3. [ ] Keith .... very good pictures.
4. [ ] My cat .... fish every day.
5. [ ] Mum and Dad .... TV at the moment.
6. [ ] Jo .... in the sea in the summer.

3 Put the verbs in brackets into the *present continuous* or the *present simple*.

1. Today, I 'm riding (ride) my bike to school.
2. In the summer, my friends .... (swim) in the sea.
3. .... Kirsten .... (make) a cake now?
4. We .... (not/do) our homework in the mornings.
5. They .... (not/run) in the park at the moment.
6. .... Hana and Jana .... (play) tennis on Tuesdays?

Progress Check 7

Listening

4 🎧55 Listen and tick (✓). There is one example.

What is Rasheed doing?

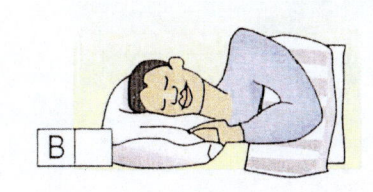

A ☐   B ☐   C ✓

1 What is Anna wearing?

A ☐   B ☐   C ☐

2 Which girl is Angela?

A ☐   B ☐   C ☐

3 What does Tom like?

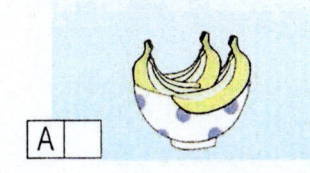

A ☐   B ☐   C ☐

5 🎧56 Song

Every year, we take our things
And go on holiday
We go to the seaside
It's a lovely place to stay
We play on the beach all day
And we swim in the sea
Oh, we love our holidays

We are swimming in the sea now
We are playing on the sand now
We are eating big ice creams now
Oh, we love our holidays

We have picnics on the beach
And we play in the sun
We build big sandcastles
And we have a lot of fun
We eat lots of ice creams
And we run and jump and play
Oh, we love our holidays

Prepositions of Place

Listen and repeat. Then act out.

Is there a rabbit in the hat?
Is there an alligator under the table?
Is there a bird on my head?
No, but there is a lion behind you!

1 Fill in: *on*, *in*, *under* or *behind*.

1 ......in...... 2 .... 3 .... 4 ....

2 Look at the picture and answer the questions.

Which animal is ...
1 in the house? ......The cat......
2 on the roof? ....
3 behind the house? ....
4 under the table? ....
5 behind the door? ....
6 on the table? ....

Prepositions of Place

3 Read and circle.

1 There is a table **in** / **on** the garden.
2 There is a dog **under** / **on** the table.
3 There are glasses **on** / **under** the table.
4 There is a bike **behind** / **on** the tree.
5 There is a ball **under** / **on** the blue chair.
6 There are apples **in** / **under** the basket.
7 There is a doll **under** / **in** the blue chair.
8 There is a cat **behind** / **on** the flowers.

4 Fill in: *on*, *in*, *behind* or *under*.

WHERE IS CARLOS?

1 He is ...*in*... the wardrobe.
2 He is .... the bed. 
3 He is .... the chair. 
4 He is .... the bookcase. 
5 He is .... the umbrella. 
6 He is .... the box.

Prepositions of Place

5 Look and fill in: *on*, *in*, *behind* and *under*.

The children are having fun in the park. Ted is 1) ...*in*... the boat. Peter is 2) .... his bike. John is sitting 3) .... the tree. Look! Ann is standing 4) .... the tree! There is a bird 5) .... the basket. Can you see the dog 6) .... the basket?

6 🎧 58 Fill in: *on*, *in*, *behind* or *under*. Listen and check.

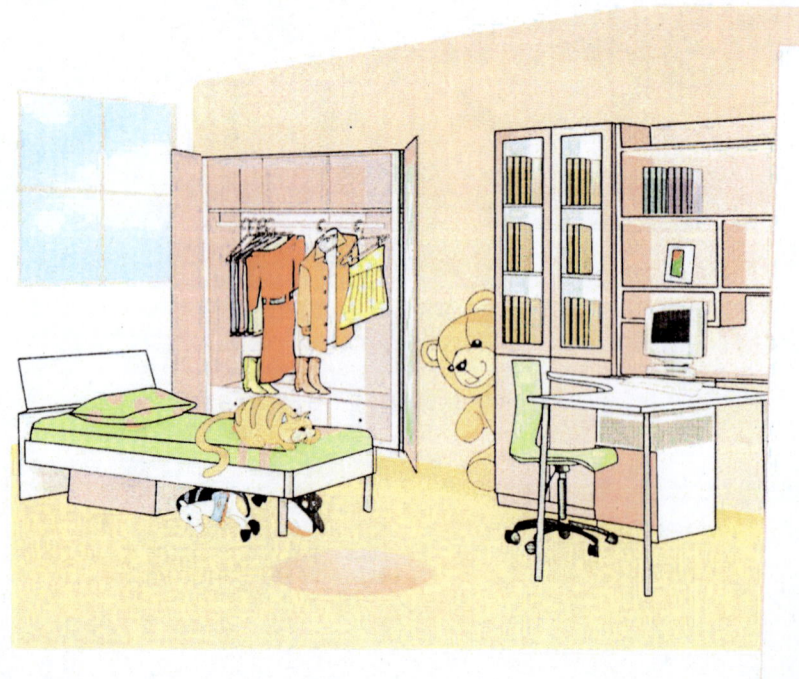

Hi! My name is Theresa and this is my room. There is a bed, a desk, a bookcase and a wardrobe 1) ...*in*... my room. There is a computer 2) .... my desk. My clothes are 3) .... the wardrobe. There are toys 4) .... my bed and a big teddy bear is 5) .... my bookcase. Peaches, my cat, is sleeping 6) .... my bed. Do you like my room?

Prepositions of Place

What is it?

Ask your partner questions and guess the animal.

Is it on the bed?

Yes, it is.

It's a lion!

Writing Activity

Write about your room. Use Exercise 6 as a model.

Hi! My name is

Prepositions of Time

Listen and repeat.

In the morning I wash my face
In the evening I clean my place
At 2 o'clock I play with my dog
At 5 o'clock I take a walk
On Wednesdays I go to the gym
On Sundays I go for a swim.

Prepositions of time

In	At	On
in the morning	at 8 o'clock	on Sunday(s), on Monday(s),
in the afternoon	at noon	on Tuesday(s), on Wednesday(s),
in the evening	at night	on Thursday(s), on Friday(s),
in July (months)	at midnight	on Saturday(s)
in (the) summer (seasons)	at lunch time	on August 2nd (dates)
in 2010 (years)	at dinner time	on Friday afternoon
	at the weekend	

1 Circle the correct prepositions.

1 I get up **at** / in 7:30.
2 August is **in** / on the summer.
3 It rains **in** / at January.
4 I go to the park on / **in** the afternoon.
5 She goes to the gym at / **on** Tuesdays.
6 We play tennis in / **on** the morning.
7 We all eat together **at** / on dinner time.
8 I watch TV on / **at** 8 o'clock.
9 We play football **on** / in Fridays.
10 We sleep **at** / in night.

2 Fill in: *in*, *on* or *at*.

1 *In* December
2 ___ Friday
3 ___ midnight
4 ___ the winter
5 ___ the evening
6 ___ 2012
7 ___ June 1st
8 ___ noon
9 ___ 11 o'clock
10 ___ August
11 ___ the spring
12 ___ Sunday

Prepositions of Time

3 Fill in: on, in or at.

1 Come to my birthday party
...on... Monday
.... 4 o'clock
.... the afternoon

2 carnival day party!
.... March
.... Saturday 15th
.... 5 o'clock

3 Food and Drink Time!
.... Friday
.... 6 o'clock
.... the evening

4 WINTER PARTY
.... December
.... Sunday 2nd
.... the morning

5 Back to school!
School starts .... September and we're celebrating with a party .... July 31st. Come to my house .... noon for a great back-to-school party!

6 The Summer is here!
Let's celebrate with a pool party .... Sunday June 30th. The fun begins .... noon and ends late .... night!

4 Match.

1. [D] Ian's birthday is on
2. [ ] The film starts at
3. [ ] She goes to school in
4. [ ] It snows in
5. [ ] I usually go to the park on
6. [ ] We sometimes visit our friends at

A the winter.
B the morning.
C the weekend.
D May 2nd.
E 7 o'clock.
F Sundays.

Prepositions of Time

5 🎧 Write the words or phrases in the correct box. Listen and check.

- 8 o'clock
- Monday
- lunch time
- the spring
- 2009
- the autumn
- Tuesdays
- the morning
- July 2010
- Friday night
- March 1st
- 7 o'clock
- midnight

on	in	at

6 Choose the correct item.

1. She eats breakfast .... the morning.
   A in   B on   C at
2. Dad comes home .... half past six.
   A on   B at   C in
3. .... Sunday we go to the beach.
   A At   B On   C In
4. We never watch TV .... dinner time.
   A in   B on   C at
5. It rains .... the winter.
   A on   B in   C at
6. My birthday is .... July 9th.
   A on   B at   C in
7. She doesn't work .... night.
   A at   B in   C on
8. We have lunch .... noon.
   A in   B on   C at
9. Chris watches TV .... the evening.
   A at   B in   C on
10. School starts .... September.
    A at   B on   C in

7 Fill in: *on*, *in* or *at*.

1. My friend's birthday is ..on.. November 3rd.
2. Lisa and Wilson usually go on holiday .... August.
3. Christopher comes home from work .... 6 o'clock.
4. She walks her dog .... the afternoon.
5. My friends and I meet .... the weekend.
6. Patricia has a piano lesson .... Friday evening.

87

Prepositions of Time

8 What does Alina do on Mondays? Use these phrases:

come back   get up   go to school   go to bed

seven o'clock    half past eight    quarter to three    quarter past nine

Alina gets up at seven o'clock.

- Now write what you do on Tuesdays.

9 Fill in: *on*, *in* or *at*.

This is Sebastian. Every day, he gets up 1) ...at... half past seven. He has breakfast and then he leaves for school 2) .... quarter past eight. 3) .... the evenings, he watches TV or reads a book. 4) .... the weekends, Sebastian likes to have fun with his friends. 5) .... Saturday, they often go to the park and ride their bikes and 6) .... the evening they go to the cinema. 7) .... Sunday morning, Sebastian and his friends usually play football.

10 Fill in: *on*, *in*, or *at*.

Dear Jessica,

It's my birthday 1) ...in... August and I'm writing to invite you to my party. The party is 2) .... Saturday August 2nd 3) .... 7 o'clock 4) .... the evening. Why don't you come 5) .... the morning so we can put up the balloons and other decorations together?

You can spend the night with us.

I really hope you can come!

Love,

Nina

Prepositions of Time

Speaking Activity

Ask and answer questions with *when* with a partner. Use the phrases: *your birthday, get up, go to school, watch TV, play football, go to the park, go on holiday.*

When is your birthday?

My birthday is in June. When do you get up?

I get up at 7:30.

GAME — What do you do?

Say a time phrase. Your partner makes a sentence using this phrase.

Tuesdays!

I go swimming in July.

I go to my guitar lesson on Tuesdays. July!

Writing Activity

It's your birthday. Write an email to your friend and ask him/her to come to your party. Use the email in Ex. 10 as a model.

Dear ....

It's my birthday ....

....

....

Love,

Who – What

🎧 61 **Listen and repeat. Act out.**

What are you doing?

I'm writing a letter.

Who is it for?

My baby brother.

But he can't read!

That's OK. I can't write!

Who – What

We use **who** for people. We use **what** for things and animals.

1 Fill in: who or what.

1 What is that?
It's a dragon.

2 .... are they?
They're my friends.

3 .... is that?
It's a bear. Run!

90

Who – What

2 Read and circle.

1 "**What / Who** is that?" "It's a mouse."
2 "**Who / What** is she?" "This is Mary."
3 "**Who / What** is this?" "It's a doll."
4 "**What / Who** are they?" "My brothers."
5 "**What / Who** are those?" "They are monkeys."
6 "**Who / What** are you?" "I'm Charlie."
7 "**Who / What** is that?" "It's my new bike."
8 "**What / Who** is he?" "My English teacher."

3 Fill in: *who* or *what*.

1 *What* are those?
They're penguins.

2 .... is she?
She's Sarah.

3 .... are they?
They're Tom and Kim.

4 .... is that?
It's a hat.

5 .... is this?
It's a robot.

6 .... is he?
He's my father.

4 Match.

1 [F] Who is she?
2 [ ] What is this?
3 [ ] What are those?
4 [ ] Who are they?
5 [ ] What is he doing?
6 [ ] Who are they talking to?

A It is a book.
B He is sleeping.
C They are John and Mary.
D Their friend, Frank.
E They are fish.
F She is Ann.

5 Write the questions to the answers. Use *who* or *what*.

1 *What is it?*
It's a dolphin.

2 ....
Miss Ross is my favourite teacher.

3 ....
I usually eat eggs for breakfast.

4 ....
The people in the photo are my friends.

5 ....
The boy in the blue T-shirt is John.

6 ....
My brother's name is Pedro.

17 Who – What

6 Fill in: *who* or *what*. Listen and check.

Sue: 1) _____ are you looking at, Jim?
Jim: A photo from my friend's costume party.
Sue: 2) _____ are you wearing?
Jim: A tiger costume.
Sue: It's funny! And 3) _____ is this behind you?
Jim: 4) _____ are you talking about? The boy in the dog costume?
Sue: No, the girl in the cat costume.
Jim: That's my friend, Mary.
Sue: 5) _____ is she doing?
Jim: She's posing for the photo!

GAME — Can you remember?

Look at the picture for one minute. Close your book and in pairs ask and answer questions with *what* and *who*.

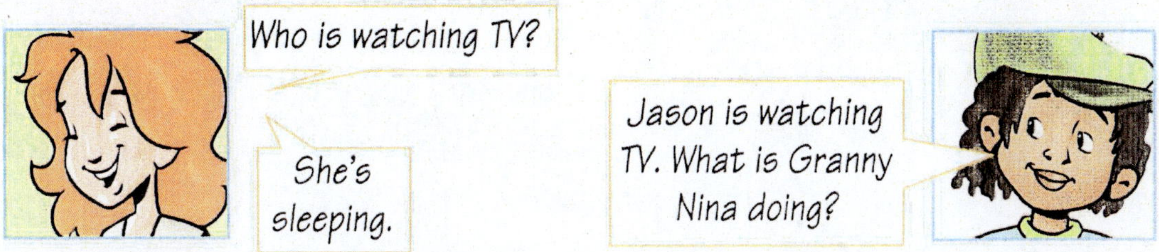

Who is watching TV?

She's sleeping.

Jason is watching TV. What is Granny Nina doing?

Progress Check 8 (Units 15-17)

1 Look at the picture. Read and circle.

1 The apples are **under** / **in** the bowl.
2 The glasses are **in** / **on** the cupboard.
3 The cat is **on** / **behind** the chair.
4 The dog is **on** / **under** the table.
5 The girl is **behind** / **on** the table.
6 The mouse is **in** / **under** the chair.

2 Write the words in the right column.

~~July~~   Tuesday   the summer   night   November 3rd
9 o'clock   the morning   noon   Monday afternoon

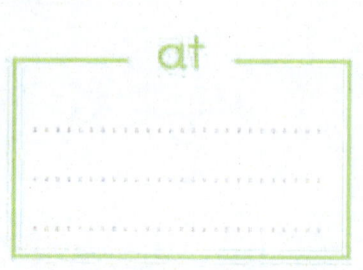

in	on	at
July		

3 Fill in: **Who** or **What**.

Sam: 1) ....'s that in your hand, Kitty?
Kitty: It's a photo. Look!
Sam: 2) ....'s that boy?
Kitty: He's my friend, Nick.
Sam: 3) ....'s that?
Kitty: It's Nick's bike. I like it very much.
Sam: 4) ....'s that girl on the bike?
Kitty: That's me.

Progress Check 8

4 Match the sentences.

1 Who are you?
2 What is that?
3 What are they doing?
4 Who are they?
5 What are these?

a They are reading.
b They are snakes.
c It is a guitar.
d I am Mrs Harp.
e They are my friends.

Listening

5 🎧 63 Listen and draw lines. There is one example.

Song

6 🎧 64

Who is in the kitchen?
Who's behind the chair?
Who is in the cupboard?
Are you hiding there?
Who's under the table?
Tell me, I can't see
Please stop hiding in the house
Come out and play with me.

Who is in the bedroom?
Who's behind the door?
Who's under the bed, now,
Hiding on the floor?
Who is in the garden?
Who's behind the tree?
It's a lovely day today
Come out and play with me.

Revision 1 (Units 1-2)

1 Fill in the missing capital letters.

A   C   G   K
        P   T
    V   Y

(Points: 18x1 18)

2 Fill in the missing small letters.

    b   e   h   j
    m   r   u
    x

(Points: 18x1 18)

3 Look at the pictures. Look at the letters. Write the words.

rain   1. ....   2. ....

3. ....   4. ....   5. ....

6. ....   7. ....   8. ....

(Points: 8x4 32)

95

Revision 1

4 Fill in: *a* or *an*.

1 ..... cat
2 ..... zebra 
3 ..... ball 
4 ..... onion 
5 ..... Indian 
6 ..... insect 
7 ..... elephant 
8 ..... star 

(Points: 8x2 — 16)

5 Circle *a* or *an*.

1 **a** / **an** frog
2 **a** / **an** umbrella 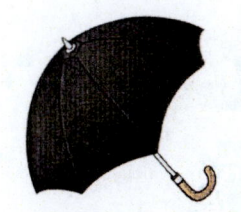
3 **a** / **an** lion 
4 **a** / **an** octopus 
5 **a** / **an** apple 
6 **a** / **an** hat 
7 **a** / **an** yo-yo 
8 **a** / **an** van 

(Points: 8x2 — 16)

(Total: — 100)

Revision 2 (Units 1-4)

1 Circle the vowels.

W j o y e l q a v u c h f i

Points: 5x1 5

2 Write the words in small letters.

1 QUEEN: ....
2 STAR: ....
3 GLASS: ....
4 HAT: ....
5 ZOO: ....

6 JAM: ....
7 FROG: ....
8 BALL: ....
9 WATCH: ....
10 TRAIN: ....

Points: 10x2 20

3 Fill in: *a* or *an*.

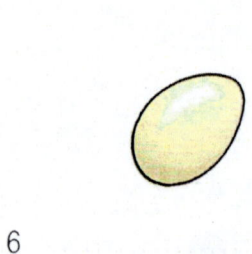

1 .... pen
2 .... cake 
3 .... alligator 
4 .... umbrella
5 .... owl 
6 .... egg
7 .... pineapple
8 .... book 
9 .... horse 

Points: 9x2 18

97

4 Write the numbers.

1 .... (33)   2 .... (49)   3 .... (12)   4 .... (58)

5 .... (13)   6 .... (62)   7 .... (100)   8 .... (84)

(Points: — 8x3 24)

5 Write the plurals.

1 car – ....
2 bus – ....
3 brush – ....
4 boy – ....

5 lorry – ....
6 lion – ....
7 watch – ....
8 zebra – ....

9 box – ....
10 snake – ....
11 glass – ....
12 baby – ....

(Points: — 12x1 12)

6 Count and write.

fish   woman   child   person   mouse   sheep   foot   tooth

three children.     1 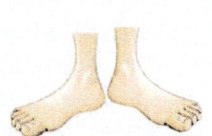 ....   2  ....   3 ....

4   ....   5 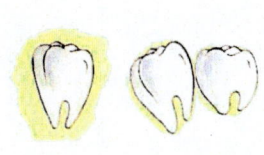 ....   6  ....   7 ....

(Points: — 7x3 21)

(Total: — 100)

Revision 3 (Units 1-6)

1 Write the words in small letters.

CHAIR　　　　　HORSE　　　　　PILOT　　　　　MELON

(Points: 4x2 — 8)

2 Fill in: *a* or *an*.

1 .... bus   4 .... ant   7 .... onion
2 .... fish   5 .... watch   8 .... glass
3 .... egg   6 .... kite   9 .... insect

(Points: 9x2 — 18)

3 Write the numbers.

1 25 ....   5 15   9   97 ....
2 48 ....   6 44 ....   10 100 ....
3 18 ....   7 89 ....
4 70 ....   8 61 ....

(Points: 10x3 — 30)

4 Write the plurals.

1 one baby – two ....   6 one fish – two ....
2 one box – two ....   7 one woman – two ....
3 one lady – two ....   8 one train – two ....
4 one child – two ....   9 one ostrich – two ....
5 one person – two ....   10 one mouse – two ....

(Points: 10x2 — 20)

99

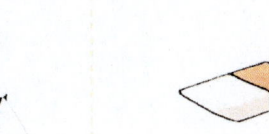

5 Fill in: *I, you, he, she, it, we* or *they*.

1  .... 2  .... 3 .... 4 ....
5  .... 6   .... 7  .... 8 .... 

(Points: 8x1 = 8)

6 Fill in: *am*, *is* or *are*.

1 I .... John.
2 We .... sisters.
3 She .... a doctor.
4 You .... a policeman.
5 It .... a lion.
6 Ben and Joe .... pilots.
7 Mark and Alan .... brothers.
8 Sarah and I .... singers.

(Points: 8x1 = 8)

7 Complete the answers.

1 Is Jasmine a teacher?
   Yes, ...
2 Are they policemen?
   No, ...
3 Are Elsa and Natasha friends?
   Yes, ...
4 Is an owl a bird?
   Yes, ...
5 Is Mark a pilot?
   Yes, ...
6 Is Debbie eleven?
   No, ...
7 Are they lorries?
   Yes, ...
8 Is Fluffy a dog?
   No, ...

(Points: 8x1 = 8)

(Total: 100)

1 Fill in: *a* or *an*.

1	ostrich	4	elephant	7	horse
2	yo-yo	5	umbrella	8	egg
3	alligator	6	monkey	9	cow

Points: 9x1 9

2 Write the plurals.

1 one cat – three ....
2 one watch – two ....
3 one child – ten ....
4 one day – seven ....

5 one box – three ....
6 one glass – four ....
7 one person – twenty ....
8 one lorry – ten ....

Points: 8x2 16

3 Look and circle the correct item.

1 he / she
2 it / they 
3 he / it 
4 it / they 

Points: 4x2 8

4 Fill in: 'm, 's or 're.

1 We .... pupils.
2 They .... dancers.
3 I .... a teacher.
4 It .... a robot.

5 He .... a policeman.
6 You .... a singer.
7 She .... an acrobat.
8 I .... a bus driver.

Points: 8x1 8

5 Underline the correct item.

1 **This / Those** is an egg.
2 **Those / That** are boats.
3 **This / These** are dresses.

4 **That / These** are trees.
5 **That / These** is a train.
6 **This / Those** is a zebra.

Points: 6x2 12

6 Fill in: *this*, *that*, *these*, or *those*.

This is a dog. 1 .... is a kite. 2 .... is an plane.
3 .... are books. 4 .... are birds. 5 .... is my dad.

(Points: 5x3 15)

7 Fill in: *have got*, *haven't got*, *has got* or *hasn't got*.

1 She .... a car. (✗)
2 They .... three cows. (✓)
3 Inga .... a blue dress. (✓)
4 We .... a boat. (✗)
5 Alexis .... a bag. (✗)
6 You .... a bike. (✓)

(Points: 6x2 12)

8 Look at the chart. Write the questions and answer them.

	horse	bike	jacket	skirt	pencil	umbrella
Has got		(✓)	(✓)			(✓)
Hasn't got	(✗)			(✗)	(✗)	

Has she got a horse? (horse)   No, she hasn't.
1 .... (bike)
2 .... (jacket)
3 .... (skirt)
4 .... (pencil)
5 .... (umbrella)

(Points: 5x4 20)

(Total: 100)

1 Read and circle.

1 The farm has two **lorry** / **lorries**.
2 Look. There's **an** / **a** helicopter.
3 The baby has got three **tooth** / **teeth**.
4 I have got **an** / **a** umbrella.
5 I can see two **fox** / **foxes**.
6 Those **man** / **men** are doctors.
7 I saw two **snakes** / **snake** in the garden.
8 That's **a** / **an** elephant.
9 The zoo has four **monkeys** / **monkey**.
10 Is this **a** / **an** lion?

Points: 10x2 20

2 Fill in: *I, you, he, she, it, we* or *they*.

1 "Is this a ball?" "No, ... isn't."
2 "Can you dance?" "Yes, ... can."
3 "Is Freddy a doctor?" "No, ... isn't."
4 "Are Luigi and Tara friends?" "Yes, ... are."
5 "Can you and Nina draw?" "No, ... can't."
6 "Has Melina got a car?" "Yes, ... has."
7 "Are .... a student?" "Yes, I am."
8 "Can penguins swim?" "Yes, ... can."

Points: 8x2 16

3 Write sentences as in the example.

These are frogs.

1 ....
2 ....
3 ....
4 ....
5 ....

Points: 5x2 10

4 Write questions then answer them. Use *can*.

Pete / read (✓) *Can Peter read? Yes, he can.*

1 Robert / ride a bike? (✗)
2 Claudia / play the piano? (✓)
3 Mr and Mrs White / drive? (✗)
4 the dog / run fast? (✓)

Points: 4x3 12

5 Write questions then answer them. Use *have got*.

Anna / a computer? (✗) *Has Anna got a computer? No, she hasn't.*
1 the children / bikes? (✓)
2 Ben and Julia / a van? (✗)
3 the dog / a house? (✗)
4 David / an eraser? (✓)

Points: 4x4 16

6 Look at the picture and write sentences. Use *There is*, *There are*, *There isn't* or *There aren't*.

ball: *There are two balls.*
1 child:
2 tree:
3 baby:
4 dog:
5 woman:
6 cat:
7 man:

Points: 7x2 14

7 Choose the correct item.

1 Julie and I ___ friends.
 A is   B are   C am

2 There are ___ in the kitchen!
 A mice   B mouse   C a mouse

3 ___ are frogs.
 A That   B This   C These

4 ___ these English books?
 A Are   B Is   C Can

5 I ___ got a basketball.
 A 'm not   B haven't   C hasn't

6 "Are you 9?" "No, I ___."
 A can't   B 'm not   C am

Points: 6x2 12

Total: 100

104

Revision 6 (Units 1-12)

1 Read and circle.

1 This is the **teachers** / **teacher's** pencil.
2 That is **an** / **a** tiger.
3 Are these your **child** / **children**?
4 This is **Sheila's** / **Sheilas'** kite.
5 Claire has got **a** / **an** yo-yo.

6 These are **womens'** / **women's** shoes.
7 Is this **an** / **a** egg?
8 He is **Tom's and Ben's** / **Tom and Ben's** dad.
9 Mr Smith is **a** / **an** astronaut.
10 These are the **boys's** / **boys'** computers.

Points: 10x2 20

2 Write: This, That, These or Those.

1 .... is a helicopter.
2 .... are oranges.
3 .... is a frog.
4 .... are planes.

Points: 4x3 12

3 Change to the plural.

She is a teacher. – *They are teachers.*
1 That is a strawberry. –
2 She is a baby. –
3 It is a mouse. –
4 This is a sheep. –

5 He hasn't got a watch. –
6 It is a monkey. –
7 There is a fox. –
8 Is that a fish? –
9 He drives a bus. –

Points: 9x2 18

4 Write the opposites.

Close the door. *Don't close the door.*
1 Don't walk!
2 Sit!

3 Talk!
4 Don't run!
5 Don't look!

Points: 5x2 10

5 Ask and answer with *can*.

1 (they/read)   2 (he/ride a bike)   3 (it/jump)   4 (she/cook)

(Points: 4x3 12)

6 Write questions then answer them. Use *have got*.

Peter / cat? *Has Peter got a cat? Yes, he has. It's his cat.*
1 Maria / orange?
2 Paul and I / camera?
3 Dad / brother?
4 You and Sue / umbrella?
5 James and Lilly / dog?
6 the monkey / banana?

(Points: 6x3 18)

7 Read and match.

B	Can you ride a bike?	A	No, he isn't.
1	Are there chairs in the kitchen?	B	Yes, I can.
2	Have they got motorbikes?	C	Yes, there is.
3	Is your dad a teacher?	D	Yes, there are.
4	Are these your books?	E	No, they aren't.
5	Is there a dog in the garden?	F	No, they haven't.

(Points: 5x2 10)

(Total: 100)

Revision 7 (Units 1-14)

1 Read and circle.

1 a / **an** elephant
2 three **houses** / house
3 a / **an** lion

4 ten star / **stars**
5 one **dish** / dishes
6 **a** / an train

7 a / **an** umbrella
8 five people's / **people**
9 one **man** / men

Points: 9x2 18

2 Fill in: This, That, These or Those.

This is a cat.   1 _____ are dogs.   2 _____ is a bird.   3 _____ are sheep.

Points: 3x2 6

3 Answer the questions.

Have you got a pencil? (✓)
Yes, I have.

1 Have you got a bike? (✗)

2 Have Mark and Mary got a car? (✓)

3 Has Jack got a jacket? (✗)

4 Has Samantha got a camera? (✗)

5 Have you got a rabbit? (✓)

Points: 5x3 15

4 Complete the sentences. Use can or can't.

Khaled	can	can't
play football	✓	
swim		✓
speak English	✓	
read	✓	
run	✓	
ride a bike		✓

Khaled **can** play football.
1 He _____ swim.
2 He _____ .
3 He _____ .
4 He _____ .
5 He _____ .

Points: 5x3 15

5 Fill in: *There is* or *There are*.

1 _____ three horses.
2 _____ a cow.
3 _____ two children.
4 _____ chickens.
5 _____ a sheep.
6 _____ a farmer.

(Points: 6x2 — 12)

6 Fill in: *my*, *your*, *his*, *her*, *its*, *our* or *their*.

1 Jake's got a camera. It's _____ camera.
2 I've got two cats. They're _____ cats.
3 She's got a radio. It's _____ radio.
4 The dog has got a ball. It's _____ ball.
5 We've got a car. It's _____ car.
6 My grandpa and grandma have got a house. It's _____ house.
7 You've got a kite. It's _____ kite.

(Points: 7x2 — 14)

7 Match the sentences to the pictures.

Look at that plane!   Don't run!   Wake up!

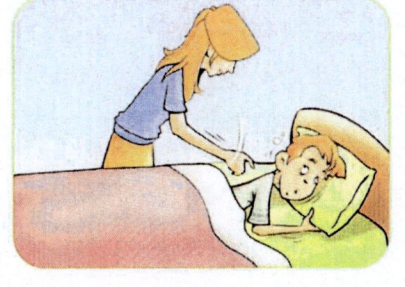

1 _____   2 _____   3 _____

(Points: 3x2 — 6)

8 Put the verbs in the brackets into the *present simple* or the *present continuous*.

Lin: Hi, Chang. What 1) _____ you _____ (do)?
Chang: Hi! I 2) _____ (make) a cake.
Lin: 3) _____ you usually _____ (cook) on Saturday?
Chang: No, I usually 4) _____ (watch) TV. Today is my sister's birthday.
Lin: Is she here? I want to wish her a happy birthday.
Chang: She isn't here now. She 5) _____ (ride) her bike in the park.
Lin: 6) _____ she _____ (like) chocolate cake?
Chang: Yes, she 7) _____ (love) it!

(Points: 7x2 — 14)

(Total: 100)

Revision 8 (Units 1-17)

1 Write sentences as in the example.

Tom / pilot *Tom is a pilot. He's a pilot.*
1 Samantha and I / sisters
2 Jenny and Tomas / seven
3 Spot / dog
4 Marisa / teacher
5 Jamal and George / firefighters

Points: 5x4 20

2 Change to the plural.

1 That is a sheep.
2 She has got a box.
3 This is a man.
4 There is a strawberry.
5 That is an ostrich.
6 There is a mouse.

Points: 6x2 12

3 Write the questions and answers.

Zak / kite
Has Zak got a kite?
Yes, he has.
It's his kite.

1 Paul and Jim / ball

2 they / bikes

3 Angela / book

4 it / fish

5 we / ice creams

Points: 5x4 20

109

Revision 8

4 Underline the correct item.

1 **Who** / **What** is the boy on the bike?
2 There **is** / **are** a man in the living room.
3 **Is** / **Are** there a cake in the fridge?
4 **What** / **Who** colour is Tom's car?
5 There **is** / **are** fish in the sea.
6 **What** / **Who** is your dog's name?

Points: 6x2 12

5 Complete the sentences. Use the *present simple* or the *present continuous*.

1 My dad .... (wash) his car every Saturday.
2 Omar .... (not/like) apples.
3 Pam .... (do) her homework now.
4 She .... (wear) a nice blue dress today.
5 Jasmine and Ann .... (not/watch) TV at the moment.
6 Anna usually .... (ride) her bike to school.

Points: 6x2 12

6 Fill in: *on, in, under* or *behind*.

1  .... 2  .... 3  .... 4 ....

Points: 4x3 12

7 Choose the correct item.

1 Do you go to the beach .... the summer?
 A on   B in   C at

2 This jacket is my ....
 A mother   B mothers'   C mother's

3 This is my dog. .... name is Jack.
 A It's   B It   C Its

4 Mr Lee is .... dad.
 A Wen's and Lin   B Wen and Lin's
 C Wen's and Lin's

5 Owls don't sleep .... night.
 A in   B at   C on

6 The party is .... Saturday.
 A on   B in   C at

Points: 6x2 12

Total: 100

Word List

A
about
add
affirmative
afternoon
again
alligator
along
alphabet
always
answer
ant
apple
arm
armchair
ask
astronaut
at
at present
at the moment
autumn

B
baby
ball
banana
basketball
bath
be quiet
beautiful
bed
bedside table
bee
behind
best friend
big
bike
bird
black
blank
blue
board
boat
boots
box
boy
bracket
breakfast
brother
brown
brush
brush your teeth
bus
bus driver

C
cake
camera
can
capital letter
car
carrot
cat
chair
check
children (pl of child)
choose
circle
classroom
climb
close
colour
column
come back
complete
computer
consonant
cook
cooker
correct
cow
cupboard
curtains
cushion
cut

D
dad
dance
dancer
date
describe
desk
dialogue
dinner
dish
do
doctor
dog
doll
donkey
door
draw
dress
drink
drive

E
ear
eat
egg
elephant
end
ending
engineer
envelope
evening
every

example
eye

F
face
fair
family
fast
feet (pl of foot)
fill in
find
firefighter
first
fish
flower
fly
football
football player
form
fox
Friday
fridge
friend
frog

G
game
get up
glass
glasses
go
grandfather (grandpa)
grandmother (grandma)
green
guess
guitar

H
hair
hand
handbag
hat
have (got)
head
he
helicopter
help
her
here
his
holiday
home
homework
horse
house

ice cream
in
in order
in pairs
Indian
insect
interrogative
it
its

J
jacket
jam
job
jump

K
kite

L
lamp
learn
lemon
letter
leg
line
lion
listen
long
long form
look
lorry (BRIT)
lunch

M
match
mechanic
melon
men (pl of man)
mice (pl of mouse)
midnight
milk
missing
Monday
monkey
monster
month
morning
motorbike
mouse
mouth
mum
my

111

Word List

name
negative
never
night
noon
nose
now
number
nurse

octopus
odd
often
on
onion
orange
ostrich
our
owl

paint
park
parrot
partner
pen
penguin
people (pl of person)
personal pronoun
picture
pillow
pilot
pineapple
pink
plane
play
plural
point
policeman
possessives
postcard
postman

prepositions of place
prepositions of time
Present Continuous
Present Simple
progress
pupil
put

queen
question

rabbit
radio
rain
read
red
remember
repeat
ride
robot
room
run

Saturday
say
scarf
schoolbag
season
sentence
she
sheep
shelf
shirt
shoe
short
short answer
short form
shower
sign
sing
singer

singular
sister
sit
skirt
sleep
small
small letter
snake
sofa
song
spring
star
story
strawberry
student
summer
Sunday
swim

talk
teacher
teeth (pl of tooth)
tennis
tennis player
that-those
their
there
they
think
this-these
Thursday
tick
tidy
today
toilet
tomato
top
towel
toy
train
trousers
truck (AM)
T-shirt
Tuesday

TV

umbrella
under
usually

van
verb
vowel

wake up
walk
wardrobe
washbasin
watch
watermelon
we
Wednesday
weekend
what
where
white
who
window
winter
women (pl of woman)
word
work
write

year
yellow
you
your
yo-yo

zebra
zoo